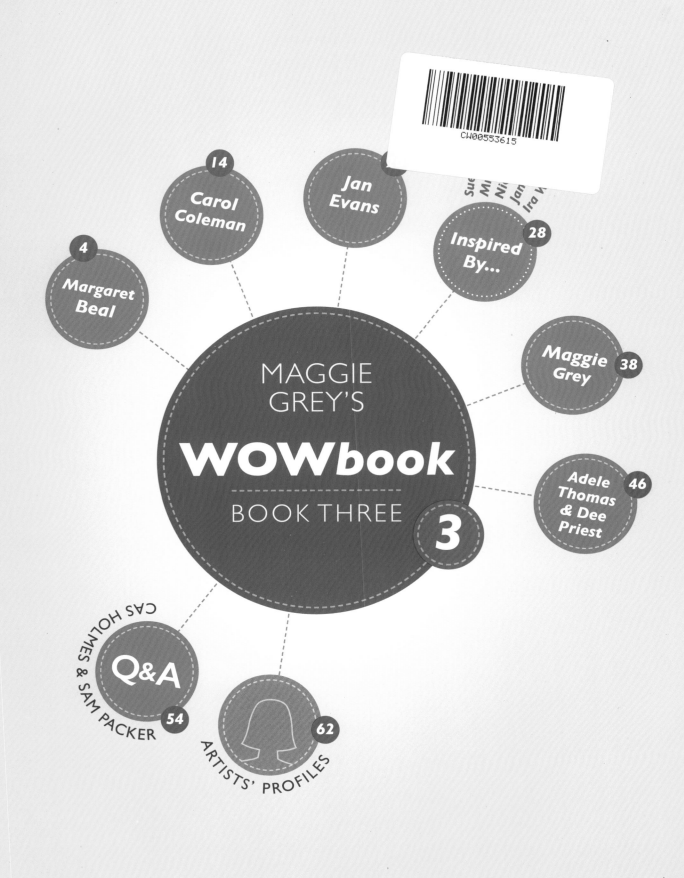

MAGGIE GREY'S

WOWbook

BOOK THREE

3

Sue M
Ni
Jan
Ira

CW00553615

Welcome *to* WOWbook **3**

BOOK THREE

I can't believe that we're now on the third WOWbook. It has proved very popular (quite beyond our expectations) and the inclusion of all the extra material on the website has led to a very lively Facebook members' group. It's such a rare thing for book authors to be able to see how their work is interpreted by others and we're especially pleased with the fact that our authors pop up on the Facebook page to answer queries – beyond the call of duty!

I'm pleased with our new series on 'Inspiration' as I find it a fascinating subject. In my own work, my starting point is almost always something I've seen at a museum, a gallery, or that eternal time-consumer, Pinterest. But, from a single starting point, the work can go in many directions; sometimes it's obvious where it's coming from, at other times I wind up so far away that the original source cannot be detected. In this book, we're inspired by the letter A. That is why we included abstract work as one of our A titles. Sue Hotchkis says that she bases her abstract work on elements such as colour, texture and surface. She describes her pieces as 'fragments saturated with colour and stitch'. I could certainly be inspired by that description. If you have a favourite artist who would fit under the letter B then let us know on our members' only Facebook group page.

Maggie Grey

> *Crackle* by Sue Hotchkis.
> H36 x W24½ x D2in (H92 x W62 x D5cm).
> Materials used are hand-dyed and screen-printed silk fabric, synthetic voile and laminated paper. Artist's own photographs manipulated using Photoshop, inkjet printed onto paper. Laminated onto voile with matt-medium and screen printed. Free machine embroidery, computerised embroidery, quilting, heat distressed and finished with appliqué.

∧ *Weim to the Rescue* by Nicky Barfoot (see Inspired by...Animals on page 32). The outline of my sketchbook drawing was transferred to fabric by tracing tissue paper onto natural linen. Stranded cotton and a variety of hand stitches were used to outline the design before 'colouring in' using straight stitches to represent feathers and fur. The Mage's cloak was cut from printed cotton and appliquéd using hand stitch. After stitching, the background was painted with acrylic paint and crayon.

SOLDERING ON
Fusing fabric

Margaret Beal

This workshop shows you ways of using a soldering iron with fabrics. If you have never used a fine-tipped soldering iron on synthetic fabric before, you will be amazed at just how useful, exciting and creative it can be. Cutting, fusing and mark-making are my three basic techniques, and combinations of all three are used throughout this workshop. The techniques are easy to learn, straightforward and fun!

BASIC TOOLS AND EQUIPMENT

- Soldering iron. Mine has a very sharp tip, 0.12 mm, and looks like a well-sharpened pencil. It uses 18 watts.
- Soldering iron stand. I use a medium-sized upturned terracotta flowerpot. The tip of the soldering iron sits safely in the drainage hole.
- Face mask. Due to the risk of breathing in toxic fumes from melting fabric, it's advisable to wear a protective face mask and work in a well-ventilated room. An extractor could also be used.
- Glass – a piece of ordinary picture glass. To avoid cutting yourself, cover the edges with masking tape.
- Fine wire wool to clean the tip of the soldering iron. I use grade 0000 to clean the tip regularly as I'm working. For ease, I push the wire wool into a small cardboard tube.
- Metal ruler – a smooth-edged metal ruler, not too narrow or you will risk burning your fingernails on the tip of the soldering iron. A mirror plate also makes a very useful small ruler and I use one all the time.
- Metal, card or wooden templates. A variety of flat metal templates can be used for cutting out shapes and for mark-making. The templates I've used for this workshop are mainly very simple geometric shapes.

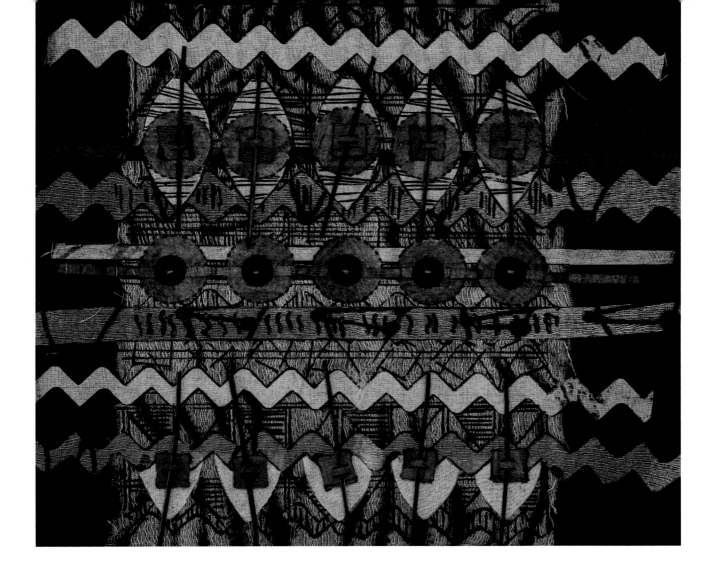

Fabrics

To begin with, the easiest fabrics to use are nylon organza and acrylic felt.

- Nylon organza is a very lightweight transparent fabric and, when pieces are layered on top of one another, a wide range of colours can be achieved.
- Acrylic felt is quite firm and compact and is ideal to use as a base fabric on which to layer the nylon organza. It comes in a variety of colours but I prefer black as marks scored into it show very clearly.
- Polyester dressmaking fabric, or charity shop finds such as scarves. I use the very soft, textured ones that have a matt surface.
- Polyester lining fabric is used sometimes as a base layer for cutting out shapes.

∧ This sampler highlights all the techniques covered in the article. The soldering iron is a wonderful tool when combined with synthetic fabrics for techniques involving cutting, fusing and mark-making.

HEALTH AND SAFETY

Some important dos and don'ts:
- Do prepare a safe surface on which to work.
- Do wear a face mask.
- Don't have extension leads on the work table.
- Don't let leads from other equipment go anywhere near the hot soldering iron.
- Always remember to switch off the soldering iron when you have finished working.
- Don't let the hot soldering iron rest on the wire wool or you will risk the wire wool catching fire.

Techniques

Cutting and fusing

This method involves placing layers of organza on top of acrylic felt and using the soldering iron to score through to the felt. It's helpful to fuse the organza layers together before placing on the felt.

1. Place two pieces of nylon organza, one on top of the other, on the glass. Layer a few small pieces of nylon organza, in a variety of colours, evenly over the top piece. Then cover these with another piece of nylon organza.

2. Place the metal ruler horizontally on the fabric about 0.5cm down from the top.

3. Slowly move the tip of the soldering iron along the edge of the ruler. This will cut through all the layers and neaten the edge at the same time. Leave the ruler in position while you remove the excess narrow strip.

4. Neaten the remaining three sides in the same way.

5. Keeping the work flat, lift it up carefully and place it on a piece of acrylic felt. Then place the work back on the glass.

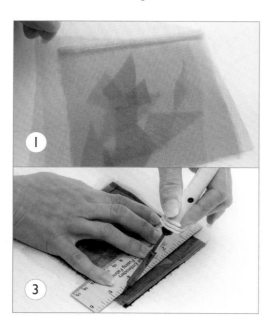

∧ This photo shows the results of cutting and fusing.

From top: A wavy strip has been cut from blue organza and fused to an organza background.

The central area shows how effective the mark-making technique can be when using rulers and templates.

At the bottom, you can see a blue circle, cut from organza, using a coin as a template, and applied to a background.

Scoring lines and patterns

It's a really good idea to make a small practice piece first. This will give you an idea of the effects that can be produced. Here is the basic mark-making technique.

1. Place the ruler horizontally on the fabric about 0.5cm down from the top.

2. Run the tip of the soldering iron slowly along the edge, as before. As you do this, the tip will score through the nylon organza and into the felt and make a visible black line (be careful not to score right through to the glass – you do not have to press hard). Then score another line, just below that one.

3. Slide the ruler down the fabric and repeat the process, scoring lines across the fabric approximately 1¼in (3cm) apart.

4. Place a template firmly on the work between the lines and run the tip of the soldering iron slowly all around the edge to score the shape into the felt. Repeat this along the width of the fabric.

5. Change the template and make your way down the length of the fabric, repeating the process between the lines and changing the template for each line as you go.

6. Using the ruler, mirror plate or a template, fill in the shapes with more pattern and lines. Try some broken lines that resemble stitching.

∨ As you can see, there are some great mark-making possibilities with this method. This looks like running-stitch.

TIP
Remember to clean the tip of the soldering iron regularly on the fine wire wool as you are working.

WARNING
Some metal shapes might get a bit hot, so be careful.

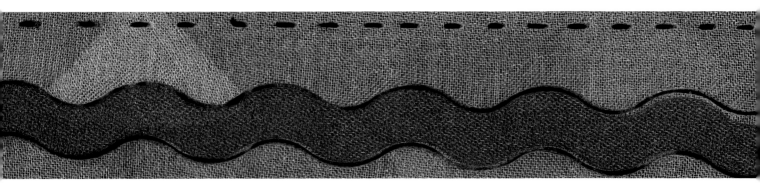

Cutting out strips and shapes

I have used mainly very simple geometric shapes.

Flat metal templates are most suitable for cutting out shapes but you can also use wooden and card ones or make your own. The metal wavy-edged rulers I bought years ago are not so easy to find now but I have also bought ones made out of card and, with practice, it is possible to cut wavy and zigzagged strips from nylon organza freehand.

When cutting out shapes, you do not have to press hard with the tip of the soldering iron but you do have to make sure that you are cutting right through to the glass. If you go too fast, the two fabrics will fuse together but will not be cut through.

Work like this

1. To cut out strips, place two or three pieces of nylon organza, one on top of the other, on the glass.

2. Place the ruler horizontally on the fabrics about 1cm down from the top of edge of the fabric. Hold it very firmly and run the tip of the soldering iron slowly along the edge, making sure that you are cutting right through to the glass. If the fabric sticks to the glass, leave everything in place and slide the ruler down and cut two more strips.

Fusing strips and shapes to the felt

Having cut out a variety of strips and shapes, you can now practise applying them to a sample that has been scored, using the ruler and template method. You can see from the photo that the cut-out shapes are fused on top of the patterns.

1. Place the scored sample on the glass and arrange the strips and shapes on top of it.

2. To fuse the straight strips to the sample, place the ruler on the long edge of a cut strip and run the tip of the soldering iron along the edge to score a line. Turn the work around and fuse the other edge in the same way.

3. Align the wavy ruler on the edge of a wavy strip and fuse it to the sample in the same way.

4. To fuse the circles, place the coin you used to cut out the shape back on top of it in exactly the same position and score very short running-stitch marks all around the very edge of it.

3. To cut out a circle, hold and press a coin firmly on the fabric, about 1cm below the last cut line, and slowly run the tip of the soldering iron all around the edge at quite an upright angle. Move the coin along the width of the fabric and cut out a row of evenly spaced circles. Once again, leave everything in place on the glass.

4. Move the ruler about 1cm below the circles and cut another straight line along the edge of the ruler.

5. Using a wavy-edged ruler, cut two or three wavy strips, one below the other.

6. Carefully lift the strips and shapes off the glass, trying not to stretch or distort them.

∨ Detail of cut-out and applied circle, showing the coin that was used as a template.

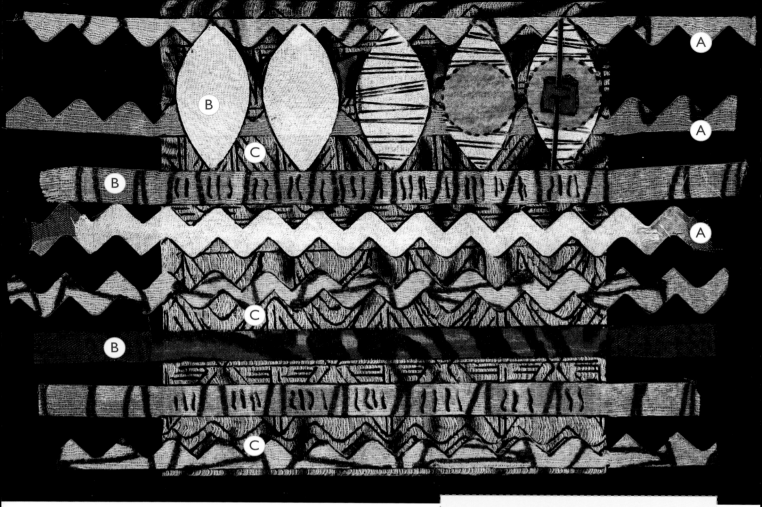

The main sampler

In this section, I have combined all the techniques we have explored and put them together in a 'sampler'. It's a great way to discover how they can all work together.

Fabrics

For this, I used a variety of polyester fabrics which were mainly scarves found in charity shops. They are very soft and have a matt-textured finish to them.

- Nylon organza is interleaved between the polyester fabrics.
- Acrylic felt is used for the base layer.
- Polyester lining fabric is sometimes used as a base fabric for cutting out shapes.

(A) **Cutting out strips**

(B) **Fusing strips and shapes to felt**

(C) **Scoring lines and patterns**

TIPS

Test the fabrics first to make sure that they are entirely synthetic by cutting through both the warp and the weft with the tip of the soldering iron.

Remember to clean the tip often as you work.

Preparing the base layer and scoring

1. Layer on the glass in the following order: one piece of acrylic felt, two pieces of nylon organza and, lastly, the polyester fabric you have chosen for the top layer. (I used black nylon organza and black felt.)

2. Holding the ruler firmly on the fabric about 0.5cm below the top edge, score a very visible row of small running-stitch marks along the edge to fuse all the layers together.

3. Move the ruler down the fabric and score more lines about 1–1½in (3–4cm) apart.

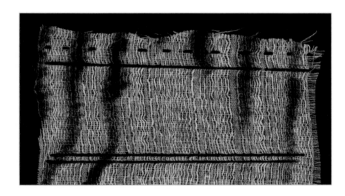

4. Using a variety of simple geometric shapes, score patterns and marks between the lines by following steps 4, 5 and 6 of the 'Scoring lines and patterns' method described on page 7.

5. Fill in the scored shapes with more patterns and marks.

Cutting out

A selection of strips and shapes were made for the sampler, following the guidelines in the 'Cutting out strips and shapes' section on page 8.

Instead of using just nylon organza, a variety of polyester fabrics were used here, both patterned and plain, on a base of two pieces of nylon organza.

To cut the shapes, place one piece of polyester fabric on top of two pieces of nylon organza on the glass, following steps 2 to 5 of 'Cutting out strips and shapes'.

1. Place the prepared base layer on the glass and fuse the strips onto it, following steps 1–3 of 'Fusing strips and shapes to the felt' on page 9.

2. Arrange the cut shapes on top of the fused strips and fuse them down by placing the template you used to cut out a particular shape in exactly the same position on top of it. Run the tip of the soldering iron all around the edge either as a continuous line or very short running-stitch marks.

3. When all the shapes are fused down over the strips, embellish some of them with more marks.
See the top row here.

4. The circles are fused down with a running-stitch mark made all around the edge of them. They also have a straight strip fused across the centre of them and another tiny black circle stitched in the centre of each one.

5. For the little red squares seen in the top and bottom rows of the finished sampler, I used two pieces of black polyester lining fabric and one piece of nylon organza for the base layers, with an interesting fabric on top. They have two little parallel slits made in the centre.

6. To make the long stiff sticks seen pushed through the slits, begin by interleaving three pieces of nylon organza between three pieces of polyester lining fabric. Finish with an interesting polyester fabric on top.

7. Starting and finishing about 1¼ in (3cm) in from the edge of the fabrics, cut several evenly spaced, long narrow strips, one below the other, by running the tip of the soldering iron slowly along the edge of the ruler. Be very sure that you are cutting right through to the glass and remember to clean the tip often.

The finished sampler

I deliberately left the beginnings and the ends of the strips on the finished sampler (see page 5), to show you the way they were layered and fused to the background. You could leave them as they are or neaten all four sides by running the tip of the soldering iron very slowly along the edge of the ruler.

I hope you enjoy trying the methods shown in this workshop. I'd love to see your work on the members' only Facebook page.

SCARBOROUGH ROCKS
Fabric and stitch collage

Carol Coleman

A day out in Scarborough when I first bought my digital camera about thirteen years ago, has produced a number of successful pieces of work. I found the sea wall south of the spa very beautiful and exhausted the batteries taking so many shots of the sandstone in the alcoves in that part of the sea front. I knew nothing about the camera (I'm notorious for not reading instructions beyond the first page) so when I loaded the images onto my laptop, I was thrilled with the clarity and colours it had recorded, using just the default setting. I have enough images from this first trip to keep me in rocks for the rest of my productive life, but I'm riveted by tree bark too.

My own work is usually created so that it looks interesting from a distance and more details are revealed as you draw closer, until the finest details can be seen up-close.

Consider how much detail you wish to add to your interpretation, but be warned – this adds a lot more time to the making of a finished piece. However, if you're having fun, time isn't important, is it?

This project is satisfyingly textural and includes hand stitching, free-machine embroidery and the use of fabric scraps that anyone can find hanging about in their workroom. It can be made as detailed or as simple as you like, accurately represented, abstract or semi-abstract.

EQUIPMENT

- Sewing machine for free-machine embroidery with appropriate foot
- Needles suitable for the kinds of thread you use; topstitch size 16 is a good all-rounder
- Light box, if you have one
- Small sharp scissors for cutting fabric
- Usual sewing requirements, including large needles to enable sewing with cords or yarns

REQUIREMENTS

- An image of rocks with interest, texture, line and colour
- Access to a computer/printer/scanner to manipulate, enhance or enlarge the image if necessary
- Lutradur (CS800)
- Cotton organdie
- Bondaweb (fusible webbing) or similar transfer adhesive
- Watercolour crayons: I used Inktense for this project but watercolour pencils would be good, too
- Threads: a collection in the colours you want to use that include hand and machine threads, yarns, cords etc. Consider any other cords or embellishments that you have in the right colours. This project used a selection of rayon and polyester threads but ordinary sewing thread is fine too.
- Fabric scraps in a profusion of colours relating to the planned work. Also check your stash for any old 'workshop wonders' as these part-finished or experimental bits and bobs will already have interesting surfaces and may come into their own on a project such as this. This is also a way to dispose of your old clothes with no one noticing.

Note on sizing It's better to work a little bigger than the standard A4 size and I will give some ideas for enlarging your photographs. The working size of mine was about 15¼in (39cm) wide with a height of 11½in (29cm) but after lacing around a board, it is now 14¾in wide (37.5cm) x 11in (28cm) high. I find this is a size that is not too big for completing a project, but big enough to give a reasonable amount of detail and colour contrast.

∧ My finished piece was based on studies of a sea wall in Scarborough. The digital image was manipulated before being traced onto fabric. The piece includes the application of fabric scraps, further defined with hand and machine embroidery.

Method

Start with your chosen digital image and examine it critically to see what changes or enhancements it might need to provide a good guide for your stitched project. In order to produce an image to work from, you may want to brighten, increase contrast, strengthen or alter colours. These options are usually available as standard for digital images. If you have more choices, then investigate those – the Posterize option can simplify a complex image and will allow you to see more clearly how you want to proceed. Try out as many variations as possible and save them all separately before you make your choice, so that you can compare the original and the enhanced versions. The original image was brightened, posterized, solarized and increased in colour values – see photo top right.

Print the image onto paper at the size you want. If you don't have an A3 printer, then crop your image in half and 'save as' two new separate images, print at A4 and tape together – see photo right.

If you want to work even larger, then divide into four quarters to print. Alternatively, have your image printed professionally at the correct size. Local copy shops sometimes offer this service at a very reasonable price. This paper copy is important to keep for reference throughout your progress as it keeps you on track and it also allows you to deviate without getting lost. I printed both the original image and the enhanced one for tracing.

Transferring the design

1. Trace your image onto the cotton organdie using watercolour crayons or pencils, leaving a border of 2–3in (5–7.5cm) for you to hold while you stitch and to give framing options at the end. A light box makes this quite easy but if you don't have one you could make some of the main features of your image stronger using an ultra-fine permanent marker to mark bolder lines on the paper copy to show through the fabric.

2. When you are satisfied with the traced image, bond the organdie onto Lutradur with Bondaweb (fusible webbing).

3. Now carefully wet the design with a fine brush, consulting the printed image to make any corrections or changes, and allow it to dry before the next stage. If the two fabrics start to separate, wait until they are dry and then iron them between two layers of non-stick parchment.

> Image traced onto organdie with watercolour crayons, bonded onto Lutradur and partially blended with water.

You should now have a good working design transferred to a thin, crisp surface that can be easily stitched, rolled and turned. This surface will resist distortion as you work with layered fabrics, adding stitching by hand and machine.

Look closely at the colours and tones in your image, then turn out your fabric scrap box and gather together everything ready for use. Try to mix all kinds of tones, textures, weights, patterns and transparencies: be a little adventurous. It's important to include a variety of tones as well as colours or your work may end up looking too bland and it is usually easier to tone down bright/strong colours with stitching than to try to brighten up a dull piece with strong, coloured stitching.

There are a number of ways to attach fabric pieces to the design. One of the easiest is to apply Bondaweb (fusible webbing) to the back of your fabric scraps and, after cutting out the bits, simply iron them in place. You could also tack them, or use tiny dabs of Pritt Stick (or a stick-type fabric adhesive) applied with a bamboo skewer.

I usually begin with the darkest areas as they often form the structure of the image and also compartmentalise areas, so it becomes easier to navigate around a complex design and recognise where you are when you turn the fabric under the machine. Begin cutting out small pieces of fabric and securing them appropriately on the surface of the organdie. You can make hand stitches at any time during this process to add texture, fine lines and to create a sense of direction as you work. If you change your mind about some bits, conceal them with a different colour if they are too difficult to remove.

If your machine allows, tighten the bobbin tension a little and slightly slacken the top tension. This will tend to keep the bottom thread underneath the fabric and only the top thread will be visible. Do try to have your bobbin colour compatible with the top surface.

At convenient intervals, machine-stitch the fabrics down, using similar-coloured thread. This will hold them down and make them secure while you continue to add more fabric. Work across the whole piece from the darkest areas to the lightest without concentrating on just one area. If you stitch too intensely in one place at a time, it will become unduly distorted. Also, as this project will be worked over several days, it's best to pause in the work after finishing a sweep over the whole piece.

∧ Apply fabric to your base and add hand stitches in the darkest areas first.

∨ All the fabric is held down with machine stitching and areas have begun to be blended in, with more stitch to shade and enhance.

∧ Some of the silver-grey areas, shown here, are made from a man's tie.

When you have finished applying the fabric pieces, blend them in with free-machine stitching. Use the direction of the stitching and fill some areas with random stitches to give different effects over the surface. When you have done this, the work may look blurred or undefined. Take time to look and decide if you want to add more hand stitching at this stage.

Then work further stitching using darker thread colours through to pale ones to add some shading and definition, and to cover up any unwanted stitches made while travelling between different areas.

It isn't always easy to know for sure when you have finished, so pause before going ahead with framing, to consider whether you are satisfied with the result. At the last minute, this piece had some sparse surface stitching added, using translucent Madeira Supertwist thread in the pale areas to suggest crystallised rock.

There are a number of options for finishing the work ready to hang. This piece was stretched over a board on top of thin wadding and laced at the back, and will sit unglazed in a 'floater' frame.

A previous similar piece was stretched over plywood, the back covered with fabric and a strip of plywood screwed to the back where I added two alternative hanging methods. I stapled a strip of Velcro to the wood and the opposite Velcro can be stapled to a batten (narrower than the picture) that is attached to the wall. Then the work is just pushed onto it. This gives the impression of no visible means of support but the disadvantage is that you need to be sure of the location and position before securing the batten — I wouldn't recommend this for very heavy or glazed work. I also attached 'D' rings to the back, so that it could be hung on a gallery hanging system, or on a domestic wall-hook with string.

Embroidery and textile art is routinely presented behind glass but this particular fabric collage is quite robust and can be enjoyed without having a barrier in front of it.

< The finished piece with all fabric sufficiently held down and bedded in. The stitches are well blended and the lines redefined.

< Consider all framing options. This piece was placed on fine wadding and stretched over a board before lacing. Here you can see the back of the piece, laced over the board.

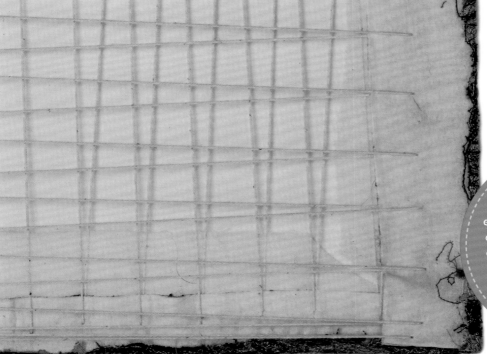

I hope you enjoy this rocky project and that it encourages you to take your camera out with you more often to record what you see – you never know where it will lead.

SPRING FORWARD
From sketch to stitch

Jan Evans

Most of my work stems from sketches and developments in my sketchbooks. I love playing around with ideas in collage and print and trying out different methods, but the initial stage of looking and drawing is the basis for what comes later.

MATERIALS

- 1 sheet of tracing paper
- 2 light-coloured Fab Foam sheets, each 12 × 18in (30 × 45cm) – available from Hobbycraft or craft shops
- 1 Fab Foam sheet with adhesive backing, 8 × 12in (20 × 30cm) – any colour
- 1 sheet of baking paper
- 2 pencils (1 soft, 1 hard)
- An old ballpoint pen
- An old brush
- A roller
- Derwent Inktense blocks
- Water spritzer
- Acrylic paints in yellows/whites/blues/greens/greys
- Calico or similar, 19½in (50cm)
- 1 sheet abaca tissue, Tissuetex or lightweight paper
- Iron-on Vilene, 6 × 6in (15 × 15cm)
- S80 Vilene 19½in (50cm)
- Small scrap of fine cotton scrim
- Textile medium – I use Vallejo
- Coloured papers/tissue – methods of colouring are shown on page 23, if you don't have any in your stash
- Sewing machine and machine threads
- Sharp scissors

In this section of the book, we'll look at a simple method of working from initial sketch to a finished stitched piece using Fab Foam sheets as printing blocks. The results are collaged and enhanced with stitch.

The landscape around my home is an ever changing inspiration. My sketch has all the characteristics of the area, the woods, winding narrow lanes flanked by hedgerows creating patterns on the hillside. These hedges are vital for our wildlife, giving shelter from the elements, a safe place to hide from predators, to build nests and find food, and a green highway connecting one area to another.

The final stitched piece is firmly based on the initial sketch, both shown opposite. This piece celebrates hedges and the wild plants that grow by the wayside and in the field margins.

Spring, I find, is a time of optimism, looking forward to warmer days and the feeling that anything is possible. The colours in the landscape are fresh, with many shades of green and an abundance of white and yellow. Queen Anne's lace is followed by cow parsley, the yellow of dandelions is superseded by golden buttercups, and growing alongside them are ox-eye daisies or moon daisies, which are a combination of all these colours.

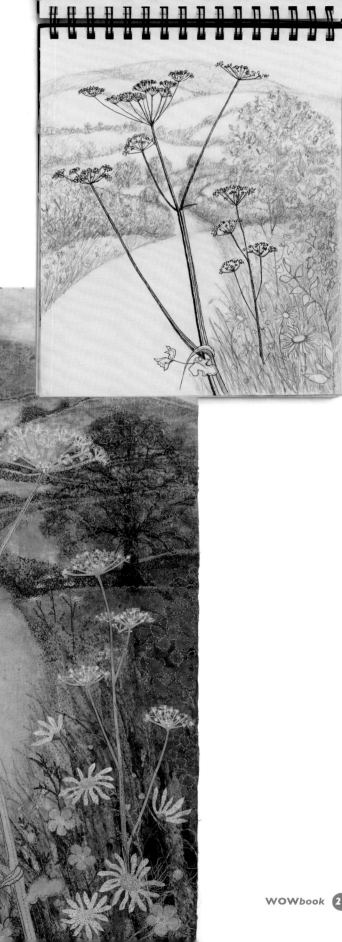

Getting started

First, make your printing mat

1. Choose a sketch or photo of a landscape and, if necessary, enlarge it on a photocopier.

2. With a sheet of tracing paper over the image, simplify by drawing the main lines with a soft pencil.

3. Turn over and transfer by re-drawing on the back with a hard pencil onto a light-coloured sheet of Fab Foam.

4. Restate these lines with an old ballpoint pen, pressing firmly to indent the foam. Note that I've used a pen with ink to show the method, but an inkless one is better. Other tools could be used such as cocktail or kebab sticks, embossing tools and even the edge of a palette knife which gives a very fine line.

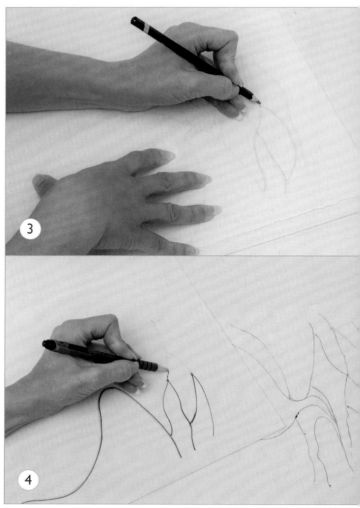

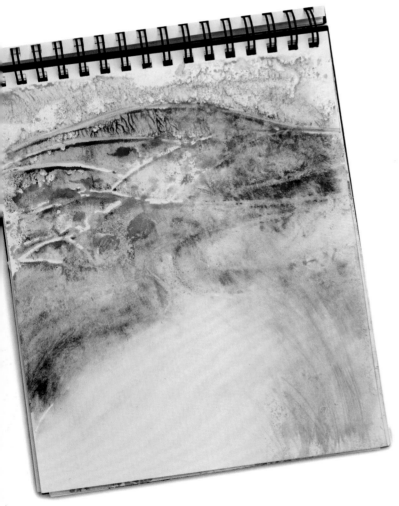

< When your printing mat is ready, I would advise you to test it out first in your sketchbook or on scrap paper. At this stage, alterations can be made by adding more lines or details.

Printing the background

1. Place a sheet of polythene over your work area.

2. Collect together your ironed fabrics and papers (the calico and abaca tissue) ready for printing.

3. Spray the mat with a little water. With a range of yellows, blues and greens, apply the Inktense sticks to the mat using the side of the sticks for more coverage. I usually break a third of the stick off in order to do this. Be bold and allow the colours to overlap and run.

4. Respray with water. Lay your paper or cloth onto the surface, smooth by hand and follow with a roller for a good print. Peel back carefully from a corner. This is a good time to check whether the lines need widening or more lines added.

5. Repeat as many times as you like for further prints.

Change the colours if you wish. You could also try overprinting onto coloured fabrics or papers, maps or text linked with your subject. I found that while the print was damp, I could blend colours with a brush on the calico surface and create more intensity of colour with the Inktense sticks. I indicated loosely where the oak tree was positioned. The indented lines revealed the colour of the background fabric and acted as a guide for stitching the hedgerows later.

Making papers

If you don't already have a stash of papers in suitable colours, try this method.

1. Take your second Fab Foam sheet and spray lightly with water.

2. Using Inktense sticks or acrylic paints and a large brush, mix and blend, dropping in contrasting colours and allowing them to run together before taking a monoprint. They are quick to produce and very useful when dry.

3. While paints are handy, take your piece of scrim and colour it in varied shades of green.

4. Leave to dry.

Printing blocks

An almost instant block can be made using adhesive-backed Fab Foam. This is what I do.

1. Draw your motif or design onto the backing paper.

2. Cut along the outline with a scalpel, craft knife or sharp scissors.

3. Peel off the backing and place onto a piece of Daler board or mountboard.

4. Trim away the excess card and place a small folded tag of masking tape on the back to act as a handle when printing.

5. Test your printing in your sketchbook or on spare paper.

55

Making flowers and cow parsley for the foreground

1. Paint your two pieces of iron-on Vilene — one yellow and one white — with acrylic paints.

2. When dry, use a pencil to draw moon daisies on the back of the white piece, bearing in mind that it will be reversed.

3. Cut out using small sharp scissors. Put on one side for later.

4. Similarly, with the yellow-painted iron-on Vilene, draw buttercup flowers on the reverse and cut out.

5. Paint the piece of S80 Vilene with a light green acrylic wash, allowing it to seep through, and leave to dry overnight.

6. Draw the stems of the large and small cow parsley on the back of the S80 Vilene. Cut out with great care, especially the fine stalks which support the florets.

Collage and print

1. Tear into some of your papers, cutting, distressing and teasing out small pieces of green scrim, and apply to the foreground using a textile medium on an old brush. A matte acrylic gel medium could be used but is stiffer when dry.

2. Leave to dry thoroughly.

3. Apply paint to your printing blocks with a large brush or roller and overprint where needed.

Before starting on the main piece, I often try out methods and techniques on spare prints in order to test out ideas.

> A small stitched sample is a good idea to see how the stitching enhances the printed fabric.

> The same scene could feature in a series showing seasonal changes. Here you can see the painted canvas ready for embellishment.

Starting to stitch

Refer to the large image of the finished piece on page 27 for details of the stitching.

1. Collect together a range of green threads from yellow-green to blue-green – light to dark. Remember that distant objects in a landscape are less distinct and slightly blurred.

2. Back your printed calico with a piece of S80 Vilene, cut to the size of your printing mat. Pin in place.

For free machining, lower the teeth, change to an embroidery or darning foot and set all dials to 0.

3. First, stitch along the unpainted lines on the hillside in light green, outwards from the centre. This anchors your cloth to the S80 Vilene. You can now remove the pins.

I use what I can only describe as a 'wriggly' stitch for building up the hedges and trees in the middle distance – yellow-greens for the sunny side, growing darker for the shaded part.

The oak tree was developed using a fairly wide zigzag stitch, randomly and freely applied in two shades of brown-green, the lighter giving the effect of sunlight catching the leaves. For the trunk, use a grey-brown thread in straight stitch.

The hedge on the left-hand side of the foreground needs some textural stitch. Do the same for the grass verge.

4. The foreground on the right can now be developed by stitching more grasses and adding moon daisies and buttercups.

5. When you are satisfied with the arrangement, cover with baking paper and iron to fix.

6. Stitch the centres of the flowers and add stalks.

The printed hedgerow leaves can be outlined in a lighter stitch to bring them forward, if necessary. It's a matter of tweaking and getting the contrasts you want.

NOTE
After a while you may find the lines on your printing mat have relaxed a little and do not print clearly. Just re-state them with your old ballpoint pen and they will be as good as new.

Final stage

The large and small cow parsley plants, at the front, are the last pieces to be applied. Lay them in place and pin when you are happy with their arrangement. The stalk of the smaller version can be held in place with stitching resembling grasses but I would advise you to change back to the basic sewing foot when stitching the large cow parsley stalk. Use a light green on the sunny side and a darker green on the shady side. The florets in both were stitched in small blocks of zigzag stitch, holding the fine stalks in place and then embellished with fine wriggles and circles of stitch to give a frothy, lacy appearance. You will find that, quite suddenly, all the hedgerows, which had seemed so dominant, recede and the picture has depth and a feeling of distance. Your work is complete!

The printing mat you have created can be used for a series based around seasonal changes, with different colours applied and the foreground details adapted. A change of colour can produce quite a different mood. Remember – these are ideas, not a prescription, and if you feel like heading off in a different direction… go for it!

> This is my finished piece where I worked from my initial sketch to this finished piece using Fab Foam sheets as printing blocks. The results are collaged and enhanced with stitch.

INSPIRED BY...

ABSTRACTS
with *Sue Hotchkis*

The core theme of my work is colour, texture and surface. It is strongly influenced by the Japanese aesthetic of *wabi-sabi*, a concept that roughly translates as appreciating the beauty in imperfection. Creating abstract forms – 'fragments' saturated with colour and stitch – is my preferred method of working and I find beauty in the breaking down of surfaces, caused by erosion and human use.

As my inspiration, I use what is often overlooked in my surroundings, providing a visual record of ageing, weathering and urban decay.

I find that inspiration almost everywhere – as long as there are elements of the man-made and nature together; throw in some neglect and you have the perfect trio. Cities are ideal, for obvious reasons. Good sources are often rundown districts, places connected with public transport – old train stations are particularly good as they are often open to the elements. However, walks in the countryside can also prove to be fruitful: old farm buildings and rusting farm machinery spring to mind. Harbours offer no end of inspiration as buildings, boats and piers battle it out with the sea.

I can find inspiration on a walk to the local shops or in exotic foreign locations but it is important to learn how to look for these things, as it is easy not to see them. Look down at worn steps, grids and overgrown painted pavements, or up at jumbled wires on telegraph poles, peeling paint on window frames or cracked, damp walls.

Preferring to use a camera rather than a sketchbook to record marks and surfaces that are in the process of breaking down, ephemeral or in a state of flux, I often come across inspiration in places where I can't (or don't) want to linger; a busy street or station can make even taking a photograph difficult at times.

As with all forms of art, whatever the subject matter, you should consider the core elements of line, space, form and composition. I look for these, as well as colour, pattern, marks and texture, and compose them within the frame of the photograph. I also take lots of shots of whatever it is I've found – both close-up and distance images. There's nothing worse than looking at the photographs at home and realising you've lost the edge of something!

I feel very excited when I find something that inspires me and can see the potential within it almost immediately, whether it's the colour, the marks, or both that can be used, either as a whole piece or just as a motif.

Once I'm home, I study the photographs I've taken of a specific place or object, selecting ones that stand out. At this point, I'm looking for potential patterns, marks, textures and colour that can be translated into a motif for stitching or a mark for printing. Some images will lend themselves straight away. In others, it might just be the colours that work together. I use Photoshop to play around with them, cropping, zooming in, altering the colours, brightness and sometimes changing them to black-and-white in order to make screens for printing. It's important to remember to save your original jpeg as well any modifications as separate files.

Occasionally, a hard copy is physically printed so that it can be taken into the print room or be studied further and used as a starting point for drawings.

Mostly, I work intuitively and often directly from the photograph – dyeing, hand painting or printing onto fabric. This result is then used to create fabric pieces and samples that can be incorporated in my finished pieces.

www.suehotchkis.com

> *Rust-rose.* H37 x W10 x D2in (H94 x W25 x D5cm).
  Materials used: felt, voile, paper, silk, digitally printed satin, and wadding. Artist's own photographs manipulated using Photoshop, inkjet-printed onto paper and digitally printed onto satin. Paper prints laminated onto voile with matt-medium and felted using an embellishing machine. Machine-stitched and heat distressed then layered and stitched using free-machine embroidery and computerised embroidery with trapunto quilting.

It's an interesting exercise to write about what inspires your own work, as such things become so ingrained in your practice you almost don't notice they are there. Looking through my textiles and fine art work, however, themes and influences keep popping up and re-emerging like old friends.

One of the biggest influences in my work is the Lincolnshire landscape. I moved to a small village with big skies and open fields seventeen years ago and nature, the changing seasons and all sorts of creatures began to appear in my stitching and painting.

Listening to music and reading are also very important for inspiring ideas. Two books that have greatly influenced my work are *The Snow Child* by Eowyn Ivey and *Women Who Run With the Wolves* by Clarissa Pinkola Estes. Fairy tales and slightly wistful characters are a recurring theme, although I never think of the story first. The characters that I create sometimes whisper their secrets to me when I've finished – but not always! I love to listen to 'Arial' by Kate Bush and Goldfrapp's 'Seventh Tree' as I work. There is something about the atmosphere these albums create that suits the way I work perfectly.

As for my creative 'home' and place of constant inspiration, it would have to be the Hope & Elvis Studio on the Welbeck Estate in Worksop. There are the most wonderful textiles and art workshops there, and the studio itself is a work of art. When I first visited, I couldn't believe how warm and welcoming everyone was. It gave me the confidence to really develop my own way of working and to focus on *Mrs Bertimus*.

I have blogged for many years and looking back on past adventures and inspirational places that I've visited can really help to kick-start an idea that may be lurking in the back of my mind. My blog is a really useful record of techniques and processes that I may have experimented with and can also give me ideas for further developments.

I suppose one slightly unusual inspiration for my work is my alopecia. I lost my hair four years ago due to stress, and being able to create art has been my way of dealing with this, which was completely out of the blue and very sudden. Stitching and painting allows me to escape into a kind of dreamland

∧ *Minuet*. This piece, as with most of my machine embroideries, was taken from a sketch. I had initially planned to just stitch the female mouse but she seemed a little bit lonely, so I adapted the sketch and added a partner for her! The base for this was a beautiful piece of antique quilt, which creates a beautifully soft surface to stitch on.

where the characters and stories come from. It was around this time that my 'rabbit girl' began to make an appearance and she still often pops up (even when I don't plan on it!). I think she must be my alter-ego but I'm not really sure. She often seems a little bit lost but she always offers me a sense of comfort and sometimes she has that twinkle in her eye! I think things that have happened to you in your life always emerge in your creative practice. I have grown to be very fond of my rabbit girl and I like the fact that I don't really understand who she is or why she's here, and that perhaps one day she will disappear…

www.mrsbertimus.blogspot.com
www.mrsbertimus.co.uk

> *Party Lurcher*. This piece was taken from a sketch and I thought that adding a party hat suited his expression perfectly! I have machine embroidered over scraps of recycled fabrics on a piece of vintage woollen blanket.

Animals have always been a big part of my life. I grew up in a house full of springer spaniels (it was a whole lot of crazy!), rabbits, hamsters and budgies and spent my teenage years at the local riding stables. When I moved into my own home, I couldn't wait to get a dog and my love affair with Weimaraners (Weims) began. My uncle had Weims and my earliest memories of the breed were of Adam, a huge beige dog (larger than me) with a big sense of humour. He had a thing for stealing underwear and running triumphantly around the house with it. From that early age, I had my heart set on owning one of these beautiful clowns.

A few years on and I share my house with my second Weim, Sas (my big beige bestie) and a sweet Jack Russell terrier called Nelly. They are both mature ladies (being in their second decades) but still full of mischief. Sas is my running buddy and constant companion (they aren't called velcro dogs for nothing) and a reminder to 'be more dog'. She is enthusiastic and embraces every opportunity. Equally, she isn't averse to lying in the garden watching insects and listening to the birds. Aside from worrying about mealtimes, not much else stresses her out. She has no concept of embarrassment, doesn't hold a grudge and always greets me like it's the best thing to have happened to her that day.

The combination of athletic prowess with noble good looks and an ability to sit upright and stare for long periods of time makes the Weimaraner an addictive muse. My Weimadog textile sculptures in their simplistic forms — seated, lying down — are inspired by their often adopted pose of vigilance, and their likeness to tribal art figures and statue guardians of ancient civilisations.

My textile pictures have a narrative behind them. I was a child of the 'Tom and Jerry' era, watching 'Top Cat' and 'Danger Mouse' (amongst other animations) and reading Richard Scarry's 'Busy Town' books. Animals, particularly dogs and cats, with varying degrees of anthropomorphism, were my superheroes. They have returned in my adult life as a playful way of observing and commenting on the more sensitive subject of human interaction. *Weim to the Rescue* is a homage to that person who is always ready to put their underpants over the top of their tights to sort out someone

∧ *Salvia* (Weimadog Sculpture). My solid textile sculptures are built up in layers, from the inside out, using hand knitted and felted fabrics. These are rolled, folded and sculpted into the desired shapes and then hand stitched to secure and add any further shaping. Once the naked sculpture is ready, I 'dress' it in knitting using the patterns, textures and shapes of the fabric, where possible, to help to reinforce the form. Reclaimed buttons are used for eyes and noses.

else's problem (see page 3). Meanwhile *Angel* is inspired by the dichotomy of good and evil. She looks sweet but also somehow sinister; it's a fine line between the two and it could go either way.

The narratives come from daily life. I love people-watching. I carry a notebook and pen in my handbag to jot down snippets from overheard public conversations and to sketch things I want to remember. Everything I make starts life in my sketchbook. I'm most creative early in the morning and I like to start my days with drawing. These are experiments, stories and things I want to remember. Mostly, they stay in the sketchbook but sometimes they ask to be stitched and the next stage begins.

More information about me and my work can be found at: *www.nickybarfoot.wordpress.com*

∧ *Angel.* My stitched pictures are created by hand with simple embroidery stitches. Tissue paper
was used to transfer the outline of my original sketchbook drawings onto natural linen (trace,
hand stitch over, rip off). I used stranded cotton and back stitch, stem stitch or running-stitch for
outlines. 'Angel' was kept as a line drawing and after stitching, the background was painted with
acrylic paint and crayon, and finished with reclaimed vintage lace and trim.

ARCHITECTURE
with *Jan Beaney*

It's a good idea to keep a small sketchbook handy when you are out and about. When one of my granddaughters was very young we would go for walks around our neighbourhood, in particular, visiting the local churches. I found them a rich source of inspiration The pencil sketches and colour notes were made in situ at St Mary's RC and Kensal Green cemeteries. The colour washes using Koh-i-Noor were added later. The tombs and mausoleums were ornately decorated and offered so many exciting design ideas.

Initially, if drawing a building causes concern, always get to know it first. Choose parts and details out of context in the first instance and really look at them very carefully.

Perhaps look at just the windows, at the outside shape and then the glass frames within. Make quick diagrams and remember to add notes on colour, texture and building materials. Follow these observations by looking at doorways, porches and the walls. What are they made of: are they made of stone, brick or are the surfaces beginning to erode? Is the plaster peeling or are they decorated with intricate carvings? One carved motif taken out of context can be a wonderful design starting point.

Roofs can be fascinating. The tiles may be arranged in a variety of ways and towers and spires can also provide good patterns to use. Ironwork often decorates ridge tiles but also can be found around gravestones; the amazing range of scrolling formations could provide so many ideas. Fine tuning your looking will reveal all sorts of new detail. Becoming aware of unexpected colour schemes, not obvious at first, can be so rewarding. Rusty iron, flaking stonework and pretty roof tiles could inspire a number of designs for a variety of techniques, not necessarily related to buildings.

Another helpful method is to draw a pattern out of context and cut out a paper shape. Use it as a template and cut out several, so a number of repeating patterns can be arranged. Always remember to butt up the shapes together to form another shape between. Background spaces can be as important as the original. Although this is a well tried design aid, it works well and can be used to inspire machine-stitched lace on soluble film for quilting and for forms of appliqué.

www.doubletrouble-ent.com

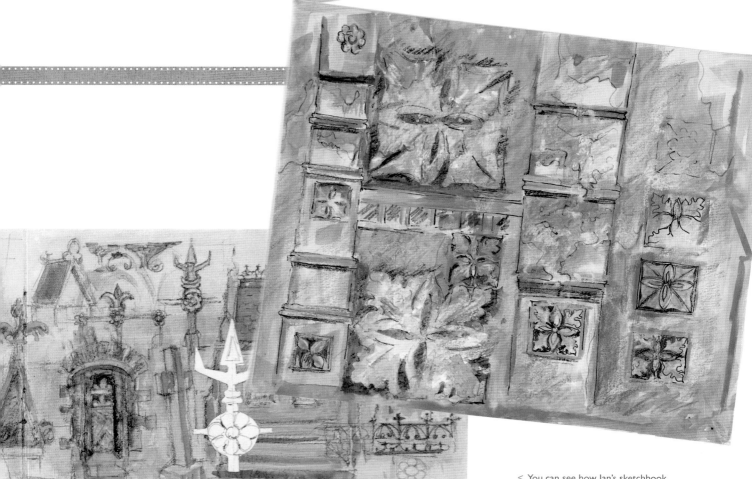

< You can see how Jan's sketchbook drawings, made on a visit to St Mary's Church and Kensal Green cemeteries, capture the shapes of windows and architectural detail. This enables further exploration of the motifs when back in the studio.

NOTE

If you want more ideas for translating inspiration into textile work, do have a look at the *Interpretations* DVD by Jan Beaney and Jean Littlejohn. It's full of ideas.

A few years ago, I had to design and make a large hanging for the Bristol Museum. It was to be part of an exhibition to celebrate the 500 years since John Cabot sailed from Bristol in the ship *Matthew* to discover new lands. He landed in North America in an area that we now call Newfoundland.

In order to glean information I had access to the museum archives, and amongst these I observed some medieval tiles that had come from Acton Court, a medieval manor house nearby.

They were the very first medieval tiles I had ever seen and I was fascinated by them. There were several drawers full of them, together with tiles from various ruined churches and abbeys around the Bristol area. I used designs from a group of the tiles as the centrepiece of a hanging, surrounding them with designs from other 15th-century items still visible in and around Bristol. They have certainly become a source of inspiration and I have discovered so much about them, from construction to design. It has never ceased to amaze me that they are still around to be discovered.

By the late 10th century, the first decorated floor tiles known in England were being made. Over the centuries, the expertise of tile-making improved in quality and in design, from the single-colour monochrome tile to the line-impressed tiles. By the 13th century, a new type of decoration was introduced. The tiler cut the entire design into a wooden stamp which was pressed into the damp clay. The resulting cavity was then filled with a white slip and the whole tile was fired in the kiln. This became the most popular type of decoration and the ones we are most familiar with. This two-colour tiling continued throughout the 13th and 14th centuries. To see collections of these and many more varieties, visit the medieval tile room at the British Museum.

In the mid 15th century, new inlaid tiles were designed for Great Malvern Priory, Worcestershire. These tiles are large and thick and, for the first time, actual dates can be seen in the decoration. The most complete set of tiles that I have seen are also laid out in the British Museum. The medieval house of William Canynge, a wealthy merchant and four times Lord Mayor of Bristol, who died in 1474, had an entire floor laid in his house (which no longer exists). The Canynge pavement is the largest surviving pavement from a medieval secular house. It is well worth a visit.

When I transfer tile designs to fabric, I use a copyright-free book of black-and-white tile illustrations and trace the designs using tracing paper. Painting the design with light and dark transfer paints and ironing onto fabric works well. If a sheer fabric is being used, it may be possible to trace through the fabric itself. Acrylic paints can then be used instead of transfer paints.

Another favourite way of using the designs is to photograph a tile or section of a tile and then take the image into an imaging program before printing it onto photo transfer paper. It can then be transferred onto fabric using a hot iron. This is a very successful method of reproduction and one I use a great deal.

www.irawoodtextileart.co.uk

> Sketchbook drawings and samples relating to architecture.

< Tiles and arches were the inspiration for Ira's work. Her research into medieval tiles resulted in sketchbook explorations and wall panels.

LEAF FALL
Needle-felting – decorative & practical

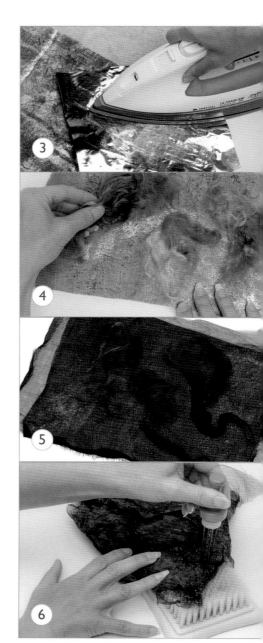

Maggie Grey

This workshop is based on needle-felting and works just as well with the felting needle and brush method as it does with the embellisher machine although, as you would expect, the latter is a little faster. The basic method is similar for both hand and machine and involves the application of silk fibres to chiffon scarves. The hand method requires the fabrics to be trapped by using Bondaweb (fusible webbing) between the layers and transfer foil can be added to this for a glitzy approach. The selvedge edges of the scarves are very useful for adding accents to the work.

YOU WILL NEED:

- Fine chiffon or nylon scarves – darker colours work best
- Bondaweb (fusible webbing) and transfer foil (for hand method only)
- Silk fibres (and/or wool fleece if making the woolly scarf version)
- Metallic machine threads for wrapped cords
- Hand-stitch threads in your colourway
- Silk cocoons, beads, acorns for decoration
- Hand felting tool, plus mat or brush for method 1 or embellisher machine for method 2
- Non-stick baking paper
- Iron

Method 1:
The hand-needled method

The hand-felting method needs to be slightly stabilised with Bondaweb. I added some transfer foil to give metallic glints but, if you're not a glitz lover, just omit this.

1. Cut off and reserve the selvedge edges of the chiffon.

2. Cover the ironing surface with non-stick baking paper. Cut two rectangles of dark chiffon and iron Bondaweb, Misty Fuse or similar adhesive webbing onto one of them, following directions on the pack, but keeping the iron temperature a little lower than recommended. Try a sample first.

3. Turn the iron to a silk setting and then iron the foil (shiny side up) onto the webbing. I prefer to use 'second use' foil with some of the surface already removed. A mix of metallic colours can look good.

4. Place silk fibres on top in leaf shapes and add another layer of chiffon on top – no foil.

5. Cover with baking paper and iron to trap the fibres.

6. Use the felting tool and needle gently all over the surface, working from the centre outwards and needling well around the leaves to trap the fibres. Needle lightly into the silk, just enough to catch it down. Keep turning the work over, lifting carefully from the brush, and needle the other side. Don't push it too hard into the brush.

7. When happy, iron again to firm the surface. Place baking paper over the top and test the iron temperature before you start – hot enough to give a flat surface but not enough to sizzle the chiffon. Pay attention to the edges around the leaves. They need to be firmly merged to trap the silk. Keep turning the fabric over as you work.

∧ *Leaf Fall.* The design was based on a waterfall, viewed through a gap between leafy trees. The needle-felted leaves form borders on each side of the 'falls', a mix of wrapped cords and pipe-cleaners, with silk cocoons and acorns providing some 'flotsam'.

Making the leaves

Now needle more heavily between the leaves in order to break up the foil. The next step is to form the shapes.

1. Pinch up the leaf shapes to define them and pin into shape, adding selvedge strips along the edges and the centres of the leaves as you go.

2. Stitch to highlight edges and veins. You can use hand or machine stitch. I have mostly worked simple running-stitch by hand.

3. Continue in this way, pinching up and stitching the shapes. You can see in the photo how the pinching and stitching adds definition (see photo above).

You will need to make two pieces of sufficient size to accommodate the 'waterfall' of wrapped threads which will fall through them. The next stage will join up with the embellisher method, so you can now skip to the next page 'Making the hanging' where this is discussed.

Method 2: The embellisher machine method

The preparation for this is similar to the hand-felted method but the silk fibres are not trapped in the same way. Because the embellisher machine method makes a more robust fabric, there is no need to iron Bondaweb and transfer foil onto the chiffon first; it's easier to add glitz in the form of threads, if you like a metallic element.

1. Cut two rectangles of dark chiffon, one larger widthways than the other. You need the selvedge hemming intact along the top and both sides.

2. Place silk fibres in a leaf shape on the base chiffon, beginning at the top right of the piece. Just make one leaf to begin with.

3. Place the other piece of chiffon – the larger one – on top, lining up the side selvedges. You will be adding the fibres as you go, poking them up under the chiffon.

4. Embellish lightly around the shape to bed it in and then, very lightly, over the leaf shape.

5. Stuff a few adjacent pockets in a similar way. Don't make them too fat. Then run the embellisher machine lightly over the surface of the silk and more heavily over the areas between to gather them up.

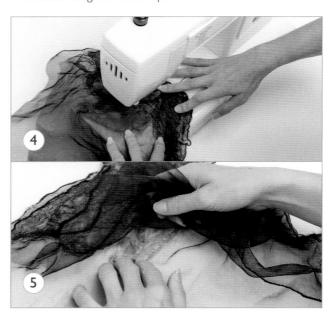

< Part way through the leaf-making process. Some of the leaves have been emphasised by needling the edge to make them stand out. There is some hand stitching here.

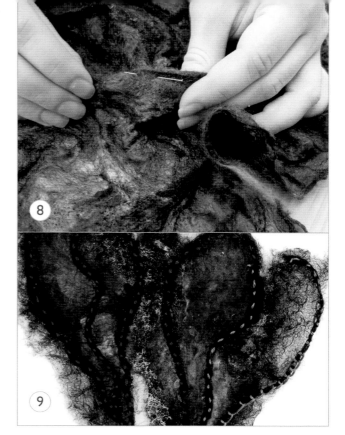

6. Continue in this fashion, making leaves and applying some of the cut-out selvedges as 'veins' down the centre and around the edges of the leaves.

7. If you like the idea of a bit of glitz, place a strip of metallic ribbon sparingly on top and embellish into the silk.

8. Pull some of the leaves into shape by folding slightly at the edges and then run the embellisher over the edges of the shape. This is a bit like 'sculpting' the piece and it should be quite three-dimensional when finished.

9. Hand stitch here and there. I rather like running-stitch in a contrasting thread.

Making the hanging

From now on, the two methods merge so, whichever you are using, you need to decide on the shape of the hanging. This needn't be a final decision as there is 'wiggle room'. The idea is to make two pieces for the hanging, with a 'waterfall' of wrapped cords, pipe-cleaners and 'vegetation' in between.

So I made two suitable shapes, one large and one small, and joined them at one end. You can see this in the photo on the right

Be prepared to make a few extra single leaves to balance the shape when you put it all together.

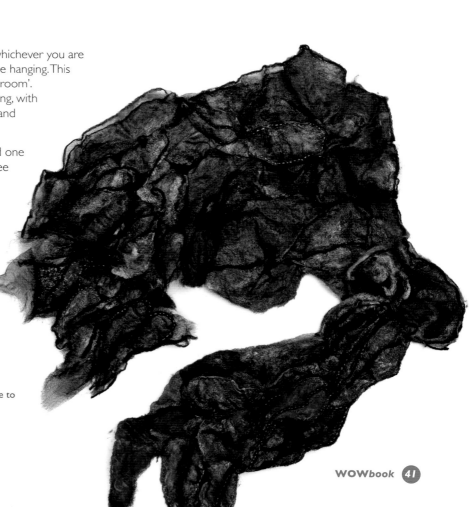

> The two pieces shown here have a gap in the centre to accommodate the river.

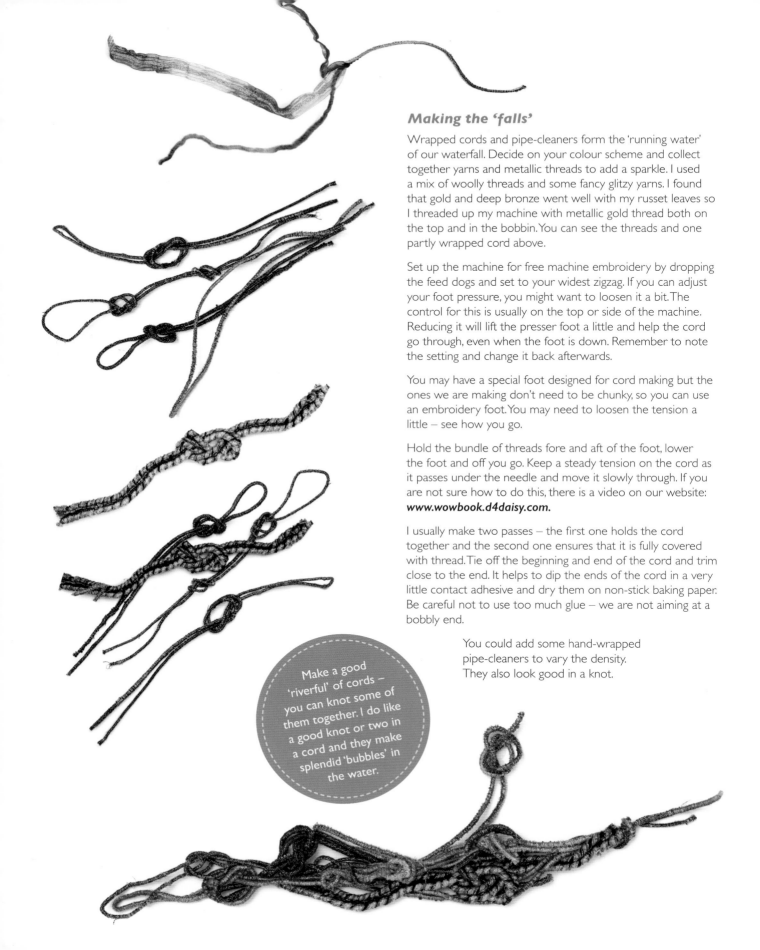

Making the 'falls'

Wrapped cords and pipe-cleaners form the 'running water' of our waterfall. Decide on your colour scheme and collect together yarns and metallic threads to add a sparkle. I used a mix of woolly threads and some fancy glitzy yarns. I found that gold and deep bronze went well with my russet leaves so I threaded up my machine with metallic gold thread both on the top and in the bobbin. You can see the threads and one partly wrapped cord above.

Set up the machine for free machine embroidery by dropping the feed dogs and set to your widest zigzag. If you can adjust your foot pressure, you might want to loosen it a bit. The control for this is usually on the top or side of the machine. Reducing it will lift the presser foot a little and help the cord go through, even when the foot is down. Remember to note the setting and change it back afterwards.

You may have a special foot designed for cord making but the ones we are making don't need to be chunky, so you can use an embroidery foot. You may need to loosen the tension a little – see how you go.

Hold the bundle of threads fore and aft of the foot, lower the foot and off you go. Keep a steady tension on the cord as it passes under the needle and move it slowly through. If you are not sure how to do this, there is a video on our website: *www.wowbook.d4daisy.com.*

I usually make two passes – the first one holds the cord together and the second one ensures that it is fully covered with thread. Tie off the beginning and end of the cord and trim close to the end. It helps to dip the ends of the cord in a very little contact adhesive and dry them on non-stick baking paper. Be careful not to use too much glue – we are not aiming at a bobbly end.

You could add some hand-wrapped pipe-cleaners to vary the density. They also look good in a knot.

Make a good 'riverful' of cords – you can knot some of them together. I do like a good knot or two in a cord and they make splendid 'bubbles' in the water.

Flotsam

You can't have a strong current of water rushing down without a certain amount of debris coming along as well. Ours will be decorative debris – here you can use your imagination. I have included silk cocoons and acorn cups rubbed with gold wax.

You could also try:
- washers, either rubbed with gold wax or painted with Pebeo Prisme paints
- eyelets stitched with gold thread on water-soluble film
- strung beads, especially metallic ones.

Knowing our readership as I do, I'm looking forward to seeing what you come up with for this section!

Putting it all together

It's worth spending some time pinning and testing to see how it looks. Arrange your leaf pieces so that the bottom one overlaps the top and then experiment with the cords, running them through the leaves so that the bottom piece covers them a little. When you are happy, stitch the cords together, as shown in the photo on the previous page.

Look at the shape of the piece and be prepared to make a few extra single- or double-leaf shapes, using your preferred method. These will be useful to drape over the cords to soften the edges or to add some surface interest and height variation when putting the piece together. Add some hand or machine stitching to these as well.

Finally add the 'flotsam' details.

Decide how it will be hung, as this may have a bearing on the shape required. Will it be left as a hanging, perhaps with a wooden batten fastened to the back? Or mounted onto a stretcher, or other firm support base, which is what I have done. This factor may determine the shape.

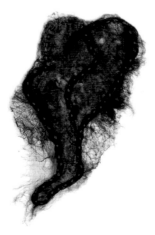

Scarf making

I fear this may be an embellisher-only method, as it's hard to persuade the chiffon and felt to knit in a satisfactory manner by hand. It is possible that nuno felting may work. I will try some experiments and report back on the website.

I had previously made woolly scarves on the embellisher machine using wool tops, wet-felting the results. They were OK, but what happened when I tried the embellisher and a chiffon scarf was something of a revelation. Having a chiffon scarf base meant that it was possible to use less wool, to felt more lightly, and have a delightfully crinkled edge. The scarves were also less itchy. They required only very light wet felting – this was more to crinkle the chiffon edges than to fix the felt.

I was also able to combine cut pieces of silk velvet as I worked. These were further embellished by hand stitching when the wet felting was done.

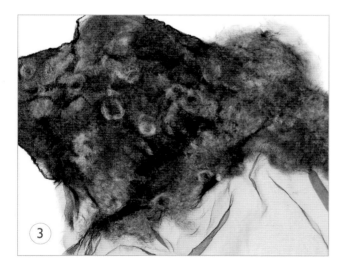

Here's the method:

Note that the chiffon scarf is used as a single layer this time – the wool is not sandwiched between the layers but laid on top.

1. Cut two or three chiffon scarves to shape, making sure that there is a selvedge along all the edges. I like pointed ends. Overlap and pin the chiffon in the middle and remove the pins as you work with the embellisher over the surface. The scarf should be slightly longer and wider than the finished requirement, as it will shrink a little in the felting. Save any cut selvedges and chiffon pieces as they are always useful.

2. Overlap the end over the middle sections so that you have a scarf shape of the required length. Run the embellisher machine over the chiffon to join the three pieces into one long scarf shape.

3. Use the embellisher machine, just as before, taking the wool right up to (but not over) the chiffon edges. Mix colours but try to blend them by putting the colour on the back and working with the machine on the front and back.

4. When all is finished and all the chiffon is covered, examine against the light and add more wool, if needed, to patch any very thin areas. Do this lightly to avoid a 'lump'. When you are happy, proceed to the felting stage.

Light felting

I find that the felting is very quick and works with the minimum of equipment, so I hope all 'proper' felters will excuse my 'fast felting' method.

You'll need a table cover, a felting bulb or a bottle with sprinkle holes and some olive oil soap, plus a couple of pieces of bubblewrap.

1. Cover your table with a waterproof table-covering and lay a towel on top.

2. Next, lay a sheet of plastic bubblewrap over the towel and put your embellished scarf on top.

3. Fill your bottle or felting bulb with warm water and sprinkle the water over the whole of your work.

4. Gently slide the bar of olive oil soap over the wet embellished piece – use very little soap.

5. Cover with another piece of bubblewrap and rub the surface well, going right up to and over the edges. When the scarf edges crinkle, you are nearly there. It shouldn't take too long as the embellisher has done most of the work already.

6. Rinse well and allow to dry, pulled into shape.

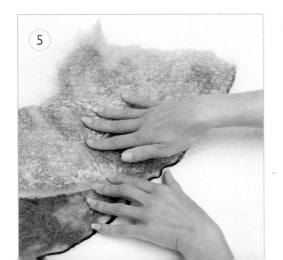

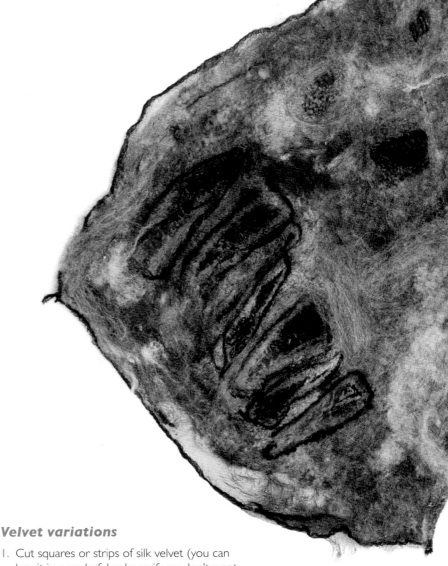

Velvet variations

1. Cut squares or strips of silk velvet (you can buy it in wonderful colours if you don't want to paint or dye it yourself). Prepare a wool-embellished surface (pre-felting) and place small squares on top – mine were about 1in (2.5cm) square.

2. Work around the edges of the square, avoiding the centre, making sure that they are well bedded into the woolly surface.

3. Felt as before. The wool should trap the velvet and you can then add some simple hand stitching to accentuate the shape. See scarf at the top of the opposite page.

∧ In the photo shown above, I used narrow rectangles of silk velvet and embellished black chiffon edges around them. This was worked as a border along the front edge of the scarf.

I'm sure that you'll all come up with some great ideas for the chiffon and felt method – can't wait to see them!

SOLAR COLLABORATION
Sun printing with SolarFast

Adele Thomas and Dee Priest

We threw down a challenge to textile artists Adele Thomas and Dee Priest. We gave them both a bottle of SolarFast – a dye that works with sunlight. We'll let Adele tell you about the basic process and then listen in as they discuss their ideas for this interesting product.

Adele: Every now and then, even an abstract enthusiast like me wants to play with photos and images. It is in our nature as artists to challenge ourselves and push into new work. I also welcome the idea of using sunlight to achieve this aim. New materials also create changes in us, so that we express ourselves differently.

I often feel homesick this time of year. The Purbeck Hills in Dorset call to me and I get a yearning to go back every spring. So, instead of fighting it, I used this desire to motivate an experiment with SolarFast. I chose Lulworth Cove, a favourite place of mine as a child. Before the holidaymakers arrive, it's a peaceful spot to sit and draw or just enjoy the margin where water meets land. The rock structure there is fascinating and it's hard to imagine solid rock being under so much pressure as to be sculpted into curved ripples.

So let's get down to business...

SolarFast is a permanent and washable, sunlight-developed dye that is used to create photographic prints on fabric or paper from a film negative. Apply SolarFast to fabric, place your negative on top, expose it to sunlight for 10–20 minutes, wash it and that's it!

Jacquard provides a negative generator (*www.jacquardsolarfast. com*) so we can turn our photographic images into film negatives for use with the dyes. To create a film negative, upload any image and convert it to black-and-white. Then invert it to create a negative, increasing the contrast to maximum. Finally, print it through an inkjet printer onto a transparent film.

DEE SAYS:
There's no preparation needed for the fabric, except to wash out any dressing. I must confess that I forgot on one piece but it still worked!

FOR THE BASIC METHOD, YOU WILL NEED:

- a high contrast image
- SolarFast dye
- SolarFast wash
- cotton fabric
- a brush or sponge
- a sheet of glass or perspex
- OHP film or acetate
- sun or UV light.

Method

1. Print the negative on transparent film using a laser or inkjet printer. Higher-contrast images work best, so put contrast up to maximum. Keep in mind that your SolarFast print will only be as good as your negative. To achieve truly white highlights on your print, for example, the darkest areas of your negative must be sufficiently opaque. Hold up your negative to a light source to make sure it is completely blocking light in its densest areas. Depending on your printer, you may need to print two negatives and layer them so the solid black areas are fully opaque. Alternatively, you may want to run the film through the printer a second time or adjust the printer settings to output more ink. I used a pen suitable for film to go over this area.

2. Place your fabric on a board or tray, so it is easy to carry outside and, using masking tape for straight edges, create a window the size of your image. Apply Solarfast to your fabric indoors (it reacts to sunlight) with a brush, sponge or old credit card. Coat the print area evenly and completely but don't soak it. You want the dye to be damp but not overly wet. Blot the fabric with a rag or paper towel to remove any excess dye before exposing. When printing on a T-shirt or garment, place a piece of paper or board between the layers to avoid bleed-through.

3. Place your negative, waterproof side down (print side up), directly onto the wet surface. For best results, place a piece of glass or acrylic over the negative. Be sure the negative is pressed flat against the wet painted surface or else you get an unclear print or shadow. I gave mine a gentle push down.

4. Expose your coated fabric to sunlight by taking it outside. Different colours require different exposure times, ranging from 10 to 20 minutes, depending on the weather conditions and the time of day. Keep an eye on your print as it changes – it's better to over-expose.

5. When you have a deep colour, bring it inside. Keep it inside until you can wash the cloth. This is important as the dye will keep reacting to sunlight.

6. Wash the print to complete the colour development and wash out any undeveloped dye. Machine wash on the hottest setting. Use SolarFast Wash for best results, but hot soapy water will do as well if you want to hand wash. Dry as normal. You can iron as this is a dye, not a transfer. The handle of the fabric will be smooth.

So that's the basic method. You will see from the finished piece on the next page that I worked the foreground flowers and added borders.

DEE SAYS:
'I was amazed at how quickly it worked – like magic!'

> This demonstrates the effects of exposure to the sun and how it produces different colours. The top sample is the one with the correct exposure level.

∧ *Cow Parsley Days*. Based on memories of heady days of sparkling water and sunshine. Sepia SolarFast on cotton was dyed with plum bark, woad, ink and rust, before hand stitching.

∨ Japanese maple leaves and bamboo on drop cloth cotton.

Adele in conversation with Dee

Adele: I know that you had equally good results, Dee, and that you tried alternative fabrics. How did that work?

Dee: I tried a number of different fabrics: space-dyed fabric, printed cotton, calico scraped with acrylic paint and dyed, white cotton sheeting and white patterned fabric – all worked to some extent. White proved the best contrast but the others worked in some ways, too. The original colour was a little bleached and the acrylic ones were very bleached. I only discovered this when I tried a piece of fabric that I had previously covered in Quink ink and bleach. It came out blue and white as well as red!

Adele: These leaf prints look good, Dee. Did you use real leaves as masks?

Dee: Yes, I loved the effects of using masks, especially on a previously painted cloth. I tried leaves, lace, Thermofax screens, stencils, painting straight on with a brush, negatives on acetate and drawing on acetate. I also tried trapping the leaves under a stencil and that worked well too – see top right.

< Experimental medley, using leaves under a commercial stencil, ground cover leaves and a twiggy plant on hand-dyed cotton.

Adele: They look great – so many possibilities. What else did you try?

Dee: My next experiment was with Thermofax screens (from Lynda Monk). These had excellent clarity and very little product was needed. They were a real success except that I got a bit excited and overlapped, resulting in blobs. As you work, the liquid seems to get thinner and travel. Also, you only have a pale image so it's hard to know where you've been until it starts to work.

Painting was next on the agenda and this was surprisingly easy to do and has many possibilities. Perhaps painting over an image? I also discovered that the Thermofax screens and painting don't need glass to work.

> Thermofax screens give a good result without glass.

Adele: I was impressed with the Jacquard tool on the website. Did you try that?

Dee: Yes, I did but, having produced a really dense black-and-white image of some tulips and printed it onto acetate, it all went slightly wrong at the printing stage. The printer put on an alarming flood of black ink, which then separated into a beautiful copper, black and clear abstract. The ink took about four days to dry and then I got one promising result. So I went back to the drawing board and tried drawing onto a polypocket with a Sharpie pen. Sadly that didn't really work. Then I tried drawing with a permanent marker on acetate. You can easily trace your drawing through the acetate and this was my best result by far.

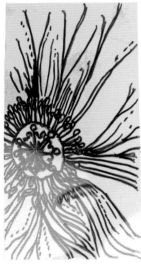

< Acetate drawn into with at least three layers of permanent pen. You can see the result in the finished piece right, where it is free-machined in white.

Adele: This raises the question of how different it is to Cyanotype, another product that works with light. Is it better, do you think?

Dee: It's definitely more versatile (and less toxic) because you can achieve different colours plus there is no preparation of the fabric and the worry of keeping it all lightfast. It actually dyes the fabric instead of coating the surface, so is more robust. Having said that, it doesn't go all the way through because of the small amount of product and the fact that you wash it all before the back is exposed. It does have a slight smell so I worked in a well-ventilated room and I wore gloves as it contains chemicals (you handle it very little).

Adele: Yes, it's really important to wash all the product out.

Dee: That's right, although I found that I didn't need a machine wash and special soap. Would I recommend this product? Yes I would! You need so little equipment and no preparation beyond getting a tray, a credit card and some glass. A little goes a long way so it is very economical. I did find that the colours mix really well.

Adele: It's interesting that we both worked in a similar way for our final pieces and I like the fact that they still look so individual – my photograph and your acetate providing the detail.

> Japanese maple leaves on richly space-dyed cotton. Kantha stitched with variegated thread and shiny machine embroidery thread.

Dee: Yes, I made a pieced hanging, using acetate and lace as a mask for the SolarFast. My borders were blocks, carved from an eraser and printed on space-dyed vintage soft cotton sheets. They were hand pieced and stitched with variegated thread.

I also made another version of the leaf prints – see right.

Adele: This is only the beginning and I know that we both have more ideas for abstracting the photographs, so the prints are less obvious. Of course, we could play around with mixing the dyes to make other colours and even laying different colours in separate areas. There is also a thickener so this can be put through a silk screen. Really we could play with overprinting images forever! I made two more pieces in a similar way with different photographs. These show experiments with all manner of resists.

< *It's Still Home, Deep Down.* Sepia SolarFast on an old cotton work shirt was dyed with woad and rust before hand stitching.

> *Pieced Memories* —
Adele Thomas.
Inspired by chalk hill
blue butterflies, bee
orchids and knapweed.
Sepia SolarFast on rust,
woad and indigo-dyed
abaca paper. This was
then machine and
hand stitched.

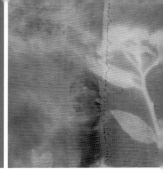

NATURE'S TRAVELLER
Cas Holmes talks to Sam Packer

Cas Holmes is one of our best loved artists, specialising in both mixed media and textile arts. She loves to create beautiful pieces using recycled and found materials. She is also well known for her collaborative ventures, such as *Tea Flora Tales* which began as an invitation to textile artists to submit work and ended with a flourish which involved the Embroiderers' Guild. Cas has been very involved in art in education, has written many books (her latest being *Textile Landscape: Painting with Cloth in Mixed Media*) and has been a good friend to us through her support of Workshop on the Web and the WOWbook.

Sam Packer is a talented textile artist who collaborated with Paula Watkins and Maggie Grey to write the book *Cut, Shape, Stitch* for d4daisy books. She has a gift for in-depth reviews and her interviews of the curators of the *Opus Anglicanum* Exhibition and of Michele Carragher, who designed and stitched the *Game of Thrones* costumes, have been widely acclaimed.

Q You say in your book, *Stitch Stories*, that: 'The motivation behind our desire to make things is as relevant as the way we make them'. By what process did you start to explore this about yourself, what were your influences and how did they come together to create your artistic identity?

A I'm not certain when I first realised or began to explore the area where the story, or idea, behind my work became the motivation for its creation, as opposed perhaps to the learning of new skills or methods. Even before I started to create things in paint and stitch, both my Romany grandmother and my painter and decorator father encouraged me to explore and look at the world around me, leading to my insatiable curiosity. My father loved a good tale and I used to meet him from work to walk, talk and look at everyday things. I grew up in Norwich in the east of England and have always been drawn to the landscape, frequently going out on bike rides in the surrounding countryside. No one who has grown up in the flat Norfolk landscape can fail to make connections between change and man's impact on the land through farming and building.

I trained in fine arts (painting) at the University of Creative Arts in Kent, UK (formerly Maidstone College of Art) and it was there I met with Janis Jefferies. Her mentorship provided not only the opportunity for me to work with various textile processes but also with the tools to reflect both positively and critically on my work. There, I began to question the connections between paper and cloth, the distinctions between textiles and painting, and to question the domestic and feminine associations often used to separate practice.

The chance came to study papermaking and textiles in Japan, a couple of years after I graduated with a Winston Churchill Award and a Japan Foundation Fellowship. This experience has had a lasting influence on my work. As I became established, exhibiting and writing, particularly for Batsford books, this gave me the freedom to express my ideas, and I've continued to hone the critical assessment of my practice. My 'artistic identity' only comes about as part of that reflection and discussion with others.

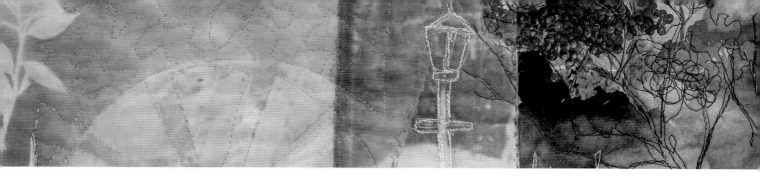

> *Blue Thistle*, part of the *40 Yards* series where Cas
looked at objects within 40 yards of her home. It
uses donated and found materials.

Q You're a prodigious sketcher; how does this process form a basis for the development of your work? Are the sketchbooks something you refer back to, or do you view them as inextricably linked to particular pieces of work and move on when completed?

A I've combined textiles with painting and drawing for over thirty years. I use sketchbooks and drawing in a number of ways – to record the things I see and to explore and challenge techniques and processes as I work through my ideas. None of my pieces is neatly planned. The visuals are not textile designs in the formal sense or plans of pieces I later make but rather an expression of the thought processes I am making, which can lead to developing ideas. My drawings exist as a means to stimulate and engage and I will often go outside as I work, to make a quick sketch, and then return to the piece in progress.

^ Sketchbook images from an Australian trip.

∨ Improvised sketchbook demo for adult education students.

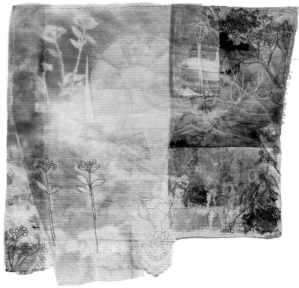

∧ Left to right: *Alphabet* and *Waterland* from the *40 Yards* series. Each of these works uses donated materials. I return to this series sporadically when I see something or am given something that brings out another element resonating with the concept.

Q What was the motivation behind the series of *40 Yards* pieces that you created? Here you look at the things within 40 yards (36 metres) of your house. Was the subject matter for each inspired by a particular response by yourself to them?

A *40 Yards* is part of an ongoing body of works which began with finding a piece of cloth outside my door with the text *40 Yards* printed on it. I decided to 'map' my locality and reflect the seasonal changes and daily observations I made of the street, gardens and park near my home in an ongoing diary piece.

It uses relevant materials gathered and is a continued exploration of the ways that travel and the domestic or home, intersect for me. It is part of a broader story in exploring the connections we have with the world around us, with issues of sustainability and the environment gently hovering in the background.

Inspiration was derived from commonplace things such as lace curtains in a window, or the thistles in my garden or the wet winter days. Botanical forms, birds and small details often crept in as a focus of calm against the disruption of time and personal space, which comes with teaching, work and family responsibilities (all of which I love most of the time). I equally became mindful of how similar references to botanical and landscape watercolour studies and fine embroidery have been perceived historically as an acceptable means of feminine craft or entertainment in the home. Since its creation and first showing at the European Patchwork Meeting in 2014, the pieces have grown and been exhibited in a variety of galleries, including an old army barracks in Parc Théodore, Monod, France, by invitation of the city of Le Mans and, more recently, at Nadelwelt. My aim is to continue the series until I have 40 yards in length. The piece also featured in my book *Stitch Stories*.

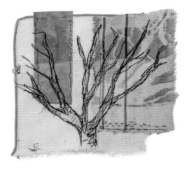

< Three *Tree Lines* studies using pieces left over from a screen-printing session and line drawings in pen. They depict the trees along a regular path taken whilst walking between Gillingham and Beccles. This road crosses the Norfolk/Suffolk border.

Q When you are travelling and away from your sewing machine, do you find that you create pieces that are different to those worked on at home? Or do you treat your travels as fact-finding missions rather than an environment for creating finished pieces? What are the essentials in your art travel kit?

A I'm interested in the concepts relating to the ideas of Japanese *wabi-sabi* (a world view centred on the acceptance of transience and imperfection) and the things often 'overlooked'. Most of the materials are found as I travel and often show signs of wear and evidence of use, which help to inform the things I make on the move. I have no clear idea where these travel pieces will lead to but do them to keep my hand in. *40 Yards* specifically evolved from this process of discovery. As part of the 'doing' I develop my ideas, yet equally some may evolve to pieces in their own right. I use whatever I have to hand for mark-making, drawing and stitch and I tend to work around the house, picking up pieces to stitch as I go.

My 'to go' kit is generally a small bag – I carry little. I usually have with me a small sketchbook, basic drawing materials, scissors, glue and standard watercolour paints or water-soluble pencils/blocks (Koh-i-Noor paints are a good alternative to watercolour and while they are not permanent, they have a lovely intense colour). I often improvise with my portable media on cloth and paper when travelling, supplemented by a few basic threads, needles, pins and scissors for hand stitching.

> Two pieces from a series based on bamboo studies. I used reclaimed indigo-dyed cloth and boro (textiles that have been mended or patched together) from Japan, and artists' ink sketches.

∧ Top: Stitch landscape sampler created as a demonstration at a Stitch Retreats course. Above: Landscape sampler in paint, cloth, paper and stitch using wallpaper (patterned and plain).

Q How did you decide on the subject matter of landscapes for your new book *Textile Landscape: Painting in Cloth with Mixed Media*? Can you tell us how the use of layering forms the basis of your approach to the creation of pieces for the book?

A I've always been interested in the connections we have with the world around us and our own take on that world. Landscape and the places where the urban and nature meet has long been my subject of choice. I started as a painter and now work in the world where both painting and cloth meet. The manipulation of cloth and found materials creates another dimension. I've always perceived what I see as indefinite. This may come from the fact I only have one functioning eye and seek to create physical layers in the work. I also believe that the impermanence of the Norfolk landscape has informed my narrative. It's a place where edges of water, land and sky merge, and the occasional line in the edge of a tree or shadow of a building draws your attention. It is that impermanence I seek, as echoed by some of the watercolours of the Norwich School or shadowy forms found in Turner's paintings. The processes I refer to in the book reflect that broad interest in application, and introduce the work of other artists who create their own response to the subject.

Q We first learned about *Tea Flora Tales* in Workshop on the Web back in 2012 when the project was launched. It has toured the world since inception and has featured in both Nadelwelt and at the Knitting and Stitching Shows in 2018. What can you tell us about this project: how has it evolved in this time and to what do you attribute its enduring appeal?

A It's fitting that *Tea Flora Tales*, which started its life at the Knitting and Stitching Show 2012, should also end with the same show in 2018, as we marked the centenary year of the end of the First World War. It began as a means to engage with visitors to my exhibition. This simple informal project gathered momentum – like a 'daisy chain' – as individuals and groups contacted me to say they would like to make a piece. In its final year, members of the Embroiderers' Guild UK provided support for the project. The simple, flexible format which encourages people to express their ideas on a teabag or small postcard-sized piece about their favourite places, is what I think has appealed. The project reflects the need to preserve our wildflowers and related habitats and raises awareness of the work of the charity *Plantlife*. Contributions continue to be received from all over the world and are added to this installation. More recently, images of poppies, cornflowers, forget-me-nots and rosemary, referencing 'peace' to be found in the landscape and natural world, have entered into the work. I'm humbled by how this small seed has grown and it seems like a stitched testament to our need to come together in sometimes turbulent times.

∧ *Tea Flora Tales*: Melanie Thompson (right) and Judith Barnett (left) from British Columbia, Canada. Both have used vintage cards or postcards.

< Examples of recent *Tea Flora Tales* including pieces by Espeth Nusser Lampe from Germany (top) and Deborah Collum (bottom left).

Q With your interest in environmental issues, do your travels around the world give you different viewpoints of the difficulties we're facing in the present day with protecting the environment and the wildlife in it? Do you find inspiration and new forms of expression for the continuing fight to preserve our natural world?

A Issues close to my heart – the threat to wildlife and wildflowers from increased urbanisation, particularly evidenced in the built-up areas where I live – continue to find their way into my work. Most of the materials I use are found or gifted from people I meet on a day-to-day basis. The history or story uncovered in a piece of cloth or paper will always provide inspiration. I find I'm still using fragments of cloth collected in Japan and India. Using found materials is the one small thing I can do in my life that can make a difference. If we all do one small thing to change what we use, what we buy and how we travel, we can all make a difference. With access to discussion groups online, people are becoming more proactive and demanding change.

Art projects and exhibitions with a focus on sustainability and environmental issues are becoming much more evident. Recent textile shows include *Stuff for Thought* organised by Heidi Drahota, first shown at the Human Rights Office in Nuremburg 2016–18, which looked at the issues of workers' rights in the textile industry; and *Keep your Eye on the Planet*, a travelling exhibition first presented at the European Patchwork Meeting in 2018 by Guldusi, a German/Afghanistan project in which artists incorporate embroideries made by Afghani women into their work for showing in group exhibitions.

www.guldusi.com/en/stick-projects.html

∨ Unfolding sketchbook which has a wallpaper bird cover.

Margaret Beal

For as long as I can remember, I had always had the urge to do something creative but lacked the confidence. When I was in my early forties and my children didn't need so much of my time, I decided to do something at the local college.

Seeing a City & Guilds Embroidery exhibition in Andover, Hampshire, UK, inspired me to give it try, so I enrolled at the local college. The design side appealed to me as much as the embroidery – I loved the course and achieved distinctions and, as a result, a piece of my Part One work was exhibited at the Commonwealth Institute.

While experimenting with mark making on woollen fabric, I accidentally used synthetic fabrics instead of natural ones! This was the 'eureka' moment because I soon realised that instead of laboriously using scissors to do all the cutwork in the border of my final piece, I could use the soldering iron instead.

My piece of work won the Visitors' Prize at an exhibition in Salisbury Museum, Wiltshire and, as a result, I was asked teach the technique at the next Salisbury Embroiderers' Guild workshop. My technique was completely original and I was then invited to do workshops for many more Embroiderers' Guilds. Over many months, I developed the cutting, fusing and mark-making techniques that continue to form the basis for all of my work and courses.

During this time, I had also started a mail order business with a fellow student. We space-dyed our own threads and sold them at various shows, our first being the Knitting & Stitching Show at Alexandra Palace, London – very brave! I continued to exhibit there for over twenty years and also at many other shows. I ran the business on my own for several years and during that time, was asked by ICHF to demonstrate at their Fashion and Embroidery Show, which was then held in Harrogate, Yorkshire. This was over twenty years ago and I'm still one of their demonstrators.

The lovely Maggie Grey, then Editor of *Embroidery* magazine, asked me to write an article. This led to more workshops in the UK and abroad, and to writing many more articles.

Following that, I enrolled on an embroidery/textile workshop with Gwen Hedley at East Berkshire College in Windsor. Gwen encouraged me to work on a larger scale, which significantly changed my approach to design and experimentation. At that time, Gwen was writing her first book for Batsford called *Surfaces for Stitch*. She asked me to write a piece on my soldering iron techniques and recommended me to Batsford.

My first book, *Fusing Fabric,* was published in 1995, becoming a bestseller, followed by my second book, *New Ideas in Fusing Fabric*, in 2013.

Website: **www.fusingfabric.co.uk**

Whilst I was studying for Part Two, I read an article in *Embroidery* magazine where someone had used a soldering iron to make singe marks on wool fabric. I decided to have a go but instead of making singe marks, my soldering iron just melted right through them.

> For the backing fabric, I layered strands of textured synthetic yarn between two pieces of very thin polyester garden fleece on a base of nylon organza. I then covered the layers with parchment paper and ironed over it. The fleece fused lightly to the yarns but when the organza figures were fused on top, and scored very lightly with fine lines, all the layers fused together very well.

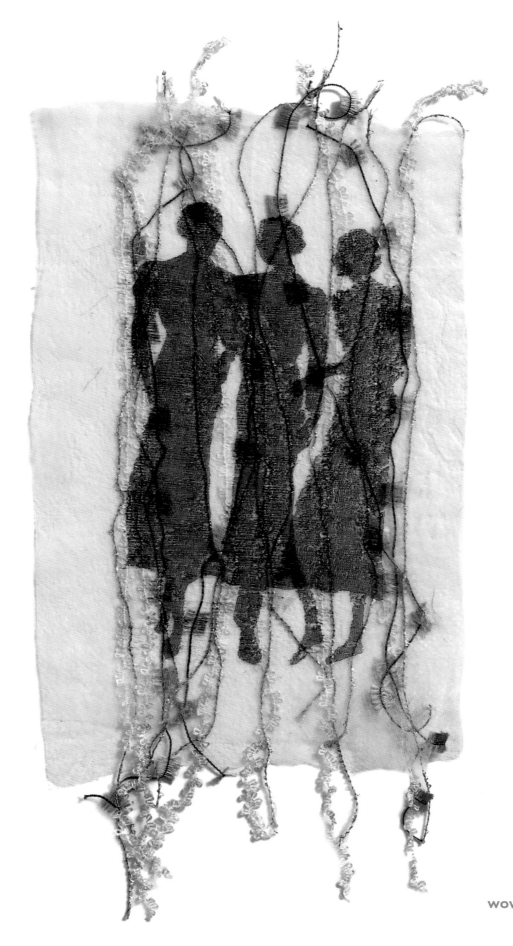

Carol Coleman

I am compulsively creative and find textiles the most versatile and satisfying medium to illustrate my inspiration. I also incorporate recycled ingredients and use paper, plastic, metal and paint within my repertoire.

My inspiration comes directly from the natural world, and my childhood fascination with rocks, fossils, shells and trees has increased now I'm able to express myself in stitched textiles. I also take inspiration from other directions: a desire to make a wearable item, a piece of beautiful fabric or thread, a challenge or exhibition theme, new materials or techniques. These all stimulate ideas to get a new project underway.

I strive to make wall-mounted work, in particular, compelling from a distance, maintaining the viewers' interest right up to the point of touch, where, occasionally, they are surprised to find they are looking at a stitched textile. My jewellery must stand scrutiny and be comfortable, robust and wearable and my boxes and coil vessels, functional.

Since moving to York in 2009, I have enjoyed involving myself with the local arts scene, joining groups and participating in mainstream open art events and opening my studio to the public. Direct contact with customers and others interested in my work at shows and in my studio has been much more enjoyable than anticipated. I'm always pleased to promote embroidery and textile art to the general public, especially when they have never before seen it used in an experimentally creative way.

I have embraced the creative tools of modern technology which have opened a new world of potential by making photography cheaper and easier. Allied with a laptop and digital projector, multiple designs can be created, stored, shared and transferred to fabric at any scale.

Using a continuous cycle of different techniques, interspersed with writing, talking, demonstrating, exhibiting and teaching, I find I'm never at a loss to fulfil creative urges. I also try to push the boundaries of what is possible with a basic sewing machine and stay open to new materials and ideas. I still need to learn more, improve my skills and master new techniques.

My jewellery has been exhibited since 2002 at *Wearable Expressions*, a juried international exhibition of wearable art in Palos Verdes, Los Angeles, USA.

I'm the author of the book *Fibredancing* and have articles published in *Stitch*, *Classic Stitches*, *Sewing World* and *Flair* magazines, and online publications *Fibre and Stitch* and *Workshop on the Web*. My work is shown in *1000 Artisan Textiles* by Sandra Salamony and Gina M Brown, and in *Experimental Textiles* by Kim Thittichai.

In 2015, I was surprised and delighted to receive the Gold Award for Textiles from *Craft & Design* magazine, where I was subsequently featured. This was a huge boost to my confidence and the realisation that my work has a wide appeal.

Website: **www.fibredance.com**

> *Slice of the Past IV.* This is my fourth piece of work taken from a photograph of a small ammonite in my fossil collection. I processed the image by intensifying the colours and transferred the design to fabric; it is stitched entirely in free-machine. It was supported on cold-water dissolving film and the edge was stitched over to create a 'free' motif.

Jan Evans

I have always loved drawing and painting and learnt to stitch from an early age, with lots of encouragement from my mother, an accomplished needlewoman, and the *Mary Thomas Book of Stitches*.

One year at Gloucester College of Art was followed by nine years as a draughtsman/tracer in a surveyors' office which demanded accurate, precise work. In my creative spare time, I designed greetings cards and wrapping papers, sold through an agent in London, made most of my own clothes and took up pottery at evening classes.

Some years later, enrolling on the City & Guilds Embroidery course reawakened my love of stitch and design, and was a great turning point. Being awarded the Silver Medal in my final year gave my confidence a boost and so I decided to enrol on the Teachers' Certificate course, with a view to sharing my love of this amazing, wonderful world of textiles and embroidery. I went on to teach City & Guilds Embroidery in Cheltenham for nine years, before leaving to concentrate on my own work.

My inspiration comes from the landscape around home, the forest, hills, fields and hedgerows of this beautiful part of Gloucestershire, UK. Local history, folklore, seasonal changes, the precious wildlife and their habitats which need protection, have all become important themes running through most of my work. A recent piece based on hedgerows has travelled as part of the very successful *DIS/rupt* exhibition by the Textile Study Group, of which I am a member. Small windows or flaps needed to be lifted by the viewer to see the animals, birds and butterflies most at risk from the changes in our countryside. By interacting with the work, hopefully, people were drawn in and would remember the message behind the piece, which was to save our hedgerows and by doing so, to save our wildlife.

I often like to work to a series or theme, immersing myself in a topic, collecting information – visual and otherwise – filling sketchbooks with drawings, paintings, collages and small stitched interpretations. I don't know why but I find it a very satisfying thing to do, and they become useful reference books not just for me but also as teaching aids. The image of *Three in a Row* was part of a series on tulips, visually exciting as a topic and having a fascinating history.

I exhibit regularly as a member of the Textile Study Group, with local art and textile groups as well as having an Open Studio every year.

You can see more about my work with the Textile Study Group here:
www.textilestudygroup.co.uk/members

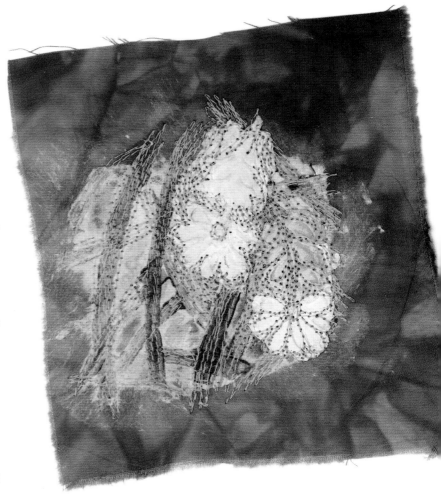

^ Another example of the print technique with hand stitching.

> *Three in a Row*. One of a series of pieces based on colourful tulips, so bright and cheering after a long, hard winter. It's on a printed calico background (using the Fab Foam method) with the tulips and leaves printed separately and applied with machine embroidery. Areas of chiffon were added to give depth and shading, attached with machine embroidery to the background.

Maggie Grey

I've always loved drawing but came to stitch when my daughter Claire was young, and inclement holiday weather led to us both buying a kit in a needlecraft shop. I recently dug out the result for a retrospective exhibition and was surprised to find it looking very vintage and, consequently, now the 'in thing'. Someone at the exhibition wanted to buy it!

A City & Guilds course in Creative Embroidery led on to teaching, both solo and with my great friend, the late Valerie Campbell-Harding. Her interest in computer design led to me dragging in my husband, Clive, as 'chief technical officer'. There was such interest in the subject that we taught it all around the world, including a memorable time in Australia, where we were based in an agricultural college and the request for an inkjet printer led to one being delivered straight from the pig-house. It smelled disgusting!

Having established ourselves with teaching, writing books for BT Batsford and editing *Embroidery* magazine for the Embroiderers' Guild, we felt brave enough to ditch our day jobs (working for an insurance company) and start a distance learning course. This became our internet magazine, *Workshop on the Web*. Having turfed out all the kids and filled their rooms with computers, we were then able actually to employ one of them to help us – and we would never have managed to keep it all going without Fiona Edwards, who now works with me on d4daisy books.

My exhibitions in the UK have included gallery shows with the exhibiting group Wessex Textiles and travelling exhibitions with the Knitting & Stitching Show. I've also exhibited in Australia and the USA and had a near sell-out show in Canada. I'm pleased that my work is held in many private collections.

I'm currently loving my distance learning classes, which are free with the WOWbooks, and take great delight in seeing students' work on our Facebook page. Another recent fun occupation for Clive and me has been making short videos for the WOWbook website.

The best things I've done in my textile working life include being part of the team developing textile modules for the Royal College of Art Schools Technology Project. I'm also proud to be President of West Country Embroiderers, a group of stitchers in the south of England. Most of all I am so glad I had the idea for the WOWbooks which have brought us great joy and I count them as the best thing I've ever done.

∨ This scarf is made by using the embellisher machine to apply wool to a nylon scarf, as described in my section of the book. The result is then lightly felted. The instructions for this are on page 44.

∧ *Mixed Metaphors.* This bag was inspired by the work of the artist, Friedensreich Hundertwasser. I love his combinations of geometric shapes and small square houses. When I made this piece, our area of Dorset had experienced severe floods, so the houses have turned into boats – on the crest of a wave. The heavy stitching on felt (designed and stitched using the embroidery unit on a sewing machine) allowed the houses in the foreground to be attached to Wireform, achieving a three-dimensional quality.

> *Doodle Birds.* Paint scraped on cotton, doodled with a fine permanent pen and free machined.

Dee Priest

I grew up in a creative family with a mother who did beautiful tailoring and a precision engineer father whose hobby was photography. It's taken me a long time to get over the precision and perfection bit! Having been scarred by needlework at school, I studied sculpture and pottery at teacher training college and went on to teach, specialising in literacy and always involving arty creativity. There were, in retrospect, several questionable and memorable lessons involving melted wax, batik and burning stuff.

It was many years before I realised that you could combine textiles, paint, paper and beads, without being perfect, and still love the result. The breakthrough really came when a textiles class by Sandra Kedzlie was advertised in a neighbouring village. I rang her and asked tentatively: 'Is it traycloths?' Sandra immediately replied 'No! Please come, this is perfect for you!' And it was.

Since then, I have dived in — attending classes, experimenting and teaching. I belong to the Exeter and District Branch of the Embroiderers' Guild where I'm a regular contributor, former Chair and South West Regional rep. I enjoy demonstrating on the Embroiderers' Guild stand at the stitching and craft shows held near Exeter. I also teach a variety of classes, mainly at Thimblestitch@Zoe's in Honiton, Devon, UK.

I exhibit with a textile group called The Woodmanton Group led by Gwen Hartley. This has really helped me to focus. My first loves are free machining, simple hand stitch, fabric and paper dyeing and painting, printing (particularly gelliplate and block printing), mixed media, challenges and anything new with possibilities! That's after focusing!

My work can be described as 'layered and colourful'. I've recently discovered a love of doodling with the machine that always seems to have hidden birds popping up.

Website: *www.facebook.com/dee.priest.79*

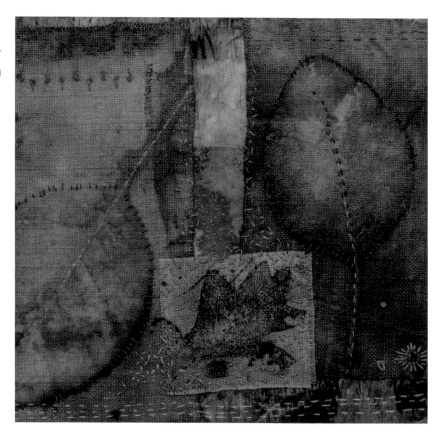

> Blackberry leaf and rust-dyed cotton/linen cloth, printed with cotinus and oak leaves and finished with hand stitching.

Adele Thomas

I was born in Poole, Dorset, UK but, for the most part, I grew up in the Purbeck area of Dorset. I took needlework as an 'O' level and failed – the only one I failed, which still amuses me! It also shows that you shouldn't stop doing something you love because an external verifier doesn't like your work. My teacher persuaded me to go to fashion college. I took a few gap years whilst raising my three daughters but it got to the point where I had to do something creative again. The call was gnawing at me.

I went on to study City & Guilds Embroidery for four years. By the end of the course, I felt far more confident but still hadn't found my visual language. I wanted my work to be more than just attractive pictures. Then I enrolled in a Fine Art degree through Plymouth University. This was the most exciting academic journey of my life. I still played around with different techniques and concepts but my ideas were becoming more focused each year. About a year after I finished my degree,

I had that long-awaited 'a-ha' moment. I finally knew what I wanted to express and how I wanted to do that.

Finally, I can say that my work is about the spiritual experience I feel when in nature. I found a wonderful word that expresses this exactly in the second year of my degree course: 'numinous' means to have a strong spiritual quality, indicating or suggesting the presence of a divinity. I started to work in only natural materials, using plant-based dyes like woad, bramble and copper. I have been experimenting with rust printing for a few years and the effect with woad has been really pleasing.

I now use stitch not just to make a mark but also including the meditative sashiko stitch for boro work, borrowing the Japanese idea of mending with stitch to create something with deeper meaning and beauty than the original.

I teach day long workshops to the Embroiderers' Guild and private groups.

Website: *www.adelethomas.co.uk*

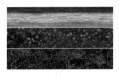